Contents

Preface

Reaching the end of the twentieth century gives us a reason to look back over the years since the Caldecott and Newbery Medal and Honor Books were established. We are impressed by how they have grown in stature to become world renown. We travel around this country and in countries around the world and are asked how the books are selected, how the awards were established, and other important questions. The books are studied to see how they reflect the times in which they were written and illustrated. And, when we review the selections from past years, we are pleased to see how well the books have withstood the test of time.

But we are not solely concentrating on the past; it is the future and the promise it holds for continued excellence in publishing the best for children. The awards were established to encourage authors, illustrators, editors, and publishers to produce the most remarkable works to stimulate the mind, satisfy curiosity, broaden horizons, and raise hope of all children. These are the same lofty goals that are in place today.

To answer the frequently asked question why the Newbery Medal is named after the Englishman John Newbery, we are reprinting with permission an article by Ronald G. Edwards. We hope when you read the essay you will gain an understanding of the importance of John Newbery to children's books.

To answer more technical and administrative questions, Bette J. Peltola's essay "Newbery and Caldecott Awards: Authorization and Terms" discusses the intricate terms and definitions that have evolved for both medals. She provides insight into the significance of the awards and also into the evaluation of children's literature. The media used in Caldecott Medal and Honor Books are updated and books have been annotated.

Finally, we include pictures of the new medalists and the committee chairs' remarks from the announcements. We hope to capture some of the excitement and enthusiasm that accompany the selection of these prize books and the presentation of the awards.

While we know the 1999 guide will be useful to you as is, we encourage your suggestions for future editions.

Susan Roman
Executive Director
Association for Library Service to Children

Newbery and Caldecott Awards: Authorization and Terms

Bette J. Peltola

ORIGINS OF THE AWARDS

Each year the Newbery and Caldecott Medals are awarded by the American Library Association for the most distinguished American children's books published the previous year. On June 21, 1921, Frederic G. Melcher proposed to the American Library Association meeting of the Children's Librarians' Section that a medal be given for the most distinguished children's book of the year. He suggested that it be named for the eighteenth-century English bookseller John Newbery. The idea was enthusiastically accepted by the children's librarians, and Melcher's official proposal was approved by the ALA Executive Board in 1922. In Melcher's formal agreement with the board, the purpose of the Newbery Medal was stated as follows: "To encourage original and creative work in the field of books for children. To emphasize to the public that contributions to the literature for children deserve similar recognition to poetry, plays, or novels. To give those librarians, who make it their life work to serve children's reading interests, an opportunity to encourage good writing in this field." The Newbery Award thus became the first children's book award in the world. Its terms, as well as its long history, continue to make it the best known and most discussed children's book award in this country.

The description of the award adopted in 1922 indicated that the Newbery Medal "is to be awarded annually to the author of the `most distinguished contribution to American literature for children,' the award being made to cover books whose publication in book form falls in the

Bette J. Peltola is professor emerita, School of Education, University of Wisconsin–Milwaukee.

calendar year last elapsed. The award is restricted to authors who are citizens or residents of the United States. Reprints and compilations are not eligible for consideration. There are no limitations as to the character of the book considered except that it be original work. It need not be written solely for children; the judgment of the librarians voting shall decide whether a book be a `contribution to the literature for children.' The award considers only the books of one calendar year and does not pass judgment on the author's previous work or other work during that year outside the volume that may be named." In 1932 the Section for Library Work with Children, with Melcher's approval, adopted the following: "To be eligible for the Newbery Medal books must be original, or, if traditional in origin, the result of individual research, the retelling and reinterpretation being the writer's own."

During the next several years, many persons became concerned that the artists creating picture books for children were as deserving of honor and encouragement as were the authors of children's books. So, in 1937 Melcher suggested a second annual medal, this to be given to the artist who had created the most distinguished picture book of the year and to be called the Caldecott Medal in honor of Randolph J. Caldecott, the nineteenth-century English illustrator. The idea for this medal was also accepted enthusiastically by the Section for Library Work with Children of ALA and was approved by the ALA Executive Board.

The Caldecott Medal "shall be awarded to the artist of the most distinguished American Picture Book for Children published in the United States during the preceding year. The award shall go to the artist, who must be a citizen or resident of the United States, whether or not he be the author of the text. Members of the Newbery Medal Committee will serve as judges. If a book of the year is nominated for both the Newbery and Caldecott Awards the committee shall decide under which heading it shall be voted upon, so that the same title shall not be considered on both ballots." In 1977 the Board of Directors of the Association for Library Service to Children rescinded the final part of the 1937 action and approved that "any book published in the preceding year shall be eligible to be considered for either award or both awards." Separate committees to choose the Newbery and Caldecott Awards were established in 1977.

ADDITIONAL CHANGES IN TERMS FOR THE AWARDS

A resolution by the Section for Library Work with Children in 1932 that "the book of a previous award winner shall receive the award only upon the unanimous vote" of the committee was later rescinded by the

Children's Services Division Board of Directors. "In view of the fact that a unanimous vote in the case of a previous winner of the Newbery or Caldecott Awards was first instituted to encourage new authors and illustrators at a period when such encouragement was needed and since such need is no longer apparent, the restriction of a unanimous vote for winning either award more than once [is] removed from terms for selection [of the awards]" (1958). In 1963 it was voted by the Children's Services Division that "joint authors shall be eligible" for the awards.

In 1978, the ALSC Board of Directors adopted new statements of terms, definitions, and criteria for each award. The new statements were prepared and adopted to provide further clarification of the basis on which the awards are to be given. They were slightly modified for further clarification in 1985 and 1987.

NEWBERY AWARD

The terms, definitions, and criteria for the Newbery Award are as follows:

TERMS

1. The Medal shall be awarded annually to the author of the most distinguished contribution to American literature for children published in the United States during the preceding year. There are no limitations as to the character of the book considered except that it be original work. Honor Books may be named. These shall be books that are also truly distinguished.
2. The Award is restricted to authors who are citizens or residents of the United States.
3. The committee in its deliberations is to consider only the books eligible for the Award as specified in the terms.

DEFINITIONS

1. "*Contribution* to American *literature*" indicates the text of a book. It also implies that the committee shall consider all forms of writing—fiction, nonfiction, and poetry. Reprints and compilations are not eligible.
2. A "Contribution to American literature for *children*" shall be a book for which children are a potential audience. The book displays respect for children's understandings, abilities, and appreciations. "Children" are defined as persons of ages up to and including fourteen, and books for this entire age range are to be considered.
3. "Distinguished" is defined as:
   - marked by eminence and distinction: noted for significant achievement
   - marked by excellence in quality

3

- marked by conspicuous excellence or eminence
- individually distinct

4. "Author" may include coauthors. The author may be awarded the medal posthumously.
5. In defining the term "original work," the committee will consider books that are traditional in origin if the book is the result of original research and the retelling and interpretation are the writer's own.
6. "American literature published in the United States" means that books originally published in other countries are not eligible.
7. "Published . . . during the preceding year" means that the book has a publication date in that year, was available for purchase in that year, and has a copyright date no later than that year. A book might have a copyright date prior to the year under consideration but, for various reasons, was not published until the year under consideration.
8. "Resident" specifies that the author has established and maintained residence in the United States as distinct from being a casual or occasional visitor.
9. The term "only the books eligible for the Award" specifies that the committee is not to consider the entire body of the work of an author or whether the author has previously won the award. The committee's decision is to be made following deliberations about the books of the specified calendar year.

CRITERIA

1. In identifying distinguished writing in a book for children:

   a. Committee members need to consider:
      Interpretation of the theme or concept.
      Presentation of information including accuracy, clarity, and
         organization.
      Development of plot.
      Delineation of characters.
      Delineation of setting.
      Appropriateness of style.

   Note: Because the literary qualities to be considered will vary depending on content, the committee need not expect to find excellence in each of the named elements. The book should, however, have distinguished qualities in all of the elements pertinent to it.

   b. Committee members must consider excellence of presentation for a child audience.
2. Each book is to be considered as a contribution to literature. The committee is to make its decision primarily on the text. Other aspects of a book are to be considered only if they distract from the text. Such other aspects might include illustrations, overall design of the book, etc.

   Note: The committee should keep in mind that the award is for literary quality and quality of presentation for children. The award is not for didactic intent or for popularity.

CALDECOTT AWARD

The terms, definitions, and criteria for the Caldecott Award are as follows:

TERMS

1. The Medal shall be awarded annually to the artist of the most distinguished American picture book for children published in the United States during the preceding year. There are no limitations as to the character of the picture book except that the illustrations be original work. Honor Books may be named. These shall be books that are also truly distinguished.
2. The Award is restricted to artists who are citizens or residents of the United States.
3. The committee in its deliberations is to consider only the books eligible for the Award, as specified in the terms.

DEFINITIONS

1. A "picture book for children," as distinguished from other books with illustrations, is one that essentially provides the child with a visual experience. A picture book has a collective unity of story-line, theme, or concept, developed through the series of pictures of which the book is comprised.
2. A "picture book for children" is one for which children are a potential audience. The book displays respect for children's understandings, abilities, and appreciations. "Children" are defined as persons of ages up to and including fourteen, and picture books for this entire age range are to be considered.
3. "Distinguished" is defined as:
    • marked by eminence and distinction: noted for significant achievement
    • marked by excellence in quality
    • marked by conspicuous excellence or eminence
    • individually distinct
4. The "artist" is the illustrator or co-illustrators. The artist may be awarded the Medal posthumously.
5. "Original work" means that illustrations reprinted or compiled from other sources are not eligible.
6. "American picture book published in the United States" specifies that books originally published in other countries are not eligible.
7. "Published . . . in the preceding year" means that the book has a publication date in that year, was available for purchase in that year, and has a copyright date no later than that year. A book might have a copyright date prior to the year under consideration but, for various reasons, was not published until the year under consideration.
8. "Resident" specifies that the artist has established and maintained residence in the United States as distinct from being a casual or occasional visitor.
9. The term "only the books eligible for the Award" specifies that the committee is not to consider the entire body of the work by an artist or whether the artist

has previously won the award. The committee's decision is to be made following deliberation about the picture books of the specified calendar year.

CRITERIA
1. In identifying a distinguished picture book for children:
    a. Committee members need to consider:
        Excellence of execution in the artistic technique employed.
        Excellence of pictorial interpretation of story, theme, or concept; of appropriateness of style of illustration to the story, theme, or concept; of delineation of plot, theme, characters, setting, mood, or information through the pictures.
    b. Committee members must consider excellence of presentation in recognition of a child audience.
2. The only limitation to graphic form is that the form must be one which may be used in a picture book (e.g., motion-picture photography is not at present possible, though still photography is).
3. Each book is to be considered as a picture book. The committee is to make its decision primarily on the illustrations, but other components of a book are to be considered especially when they make a book less effective as a children's picture book. Such other components might include the written text, the overall design of the book, etc.

Note: The committee should keep in mind that the award is for distinguished illustrations in a picture book and for excellence of pictorial presentation for children. The award is not for didactic intent or for popularity.

AWARD COMMITTEES

The committees that select the Newbery and the Caldecott Medal and Honor Books each have fifteen members including the chair. The ALSC membership elects the chair and seven members from a slate drawn up by the nominating committee; the ALSC president-elect appoints the remaining seven members. All members of the committees are members of ALSC.

During the year, each committee member reads as many of the eligible books as possible, including all books suggested by other committee members and by other members of ALSC. Twice in the autumn, committee members cast preliminary ballots to begin to focus attention on the books likely to be of most interest in the selection discussions. No eligible book which has been suggested before the midwinter selection meetings is excluded from consideration, however, even if it was not nominated on a preliminary ballot. During the selection meetings, the committee discusses all nominated and suggested books before beginning balloting. Each committee member votes for three books, with four points assigned to first choice, three to second, and two to third choice. To win, a book must receive at least eight first place choices and at least eight points more than any other book. Once a winner is chosen, the committee decides whether to name honor books and how many.

DESCRIPTION OF THE MEDALS

In 1921 Melcher had the Newbery Medal designed by René Paul Chambellan. In 1937 Chambellan designed the Caldecott Medal. The bronze medals, shown below, have the winner's name and the date engraved on the back. The ALA Executive Board in 1922 delegated to the Children's Librarians' Section the responsibility for selecting the book to receive the Newbery Medal. The inscription on the Newbery Medal still reads "Children's Librarians' Section," although the section has changed its name four times and its membership now includes both school and public library children's librarians in contrast to the years 1922–58, when the section, under three different names, included only public library children's librarians. (The section names: until 1929, Children's Librarians' Section; 1929–42, Section for Library Work with Children; 1942–58,

JOHN NEWBERY MEDAL

THE CALDECOTT MEDAL

Children's Library Association; 1958–77, Children's Service Division; and, Association for Library Service to Children (ALSC), 1977 to date.)

When the Caldecott Medal was accepted in 1937, the Section for Library Work with Children invited the School Libraries Section (now American Association of School Librarians) to name five of its members to the awards committee each year. For this reason the Caldecott Medal inscription reads: "Awarded annually by the Children's and School Librarians Sections of the American Library Association." This is a combination and simplification of the actual names of the sections. The wording continues even though several ALA reorganizations resulted in 1958 in the present divisions, among them the Children's Services Division (now the Association for Library Service to Children), made up of public library children's librarians, school librarians, and others interested in children's library services and good books for children. In 1958 the Children's Services Division Board of Directors recognized that the wording on both medals was incorrect in terms of current ALA terminology. It realized that confusion about the membership of the committee that chooses the medal winners could result from the discrepancies. However, the CSD board decided to request no change in the inscription on either medal, preferring to have them continue in their original form and design. Responsibility for both awards resides with ALSC, formerly the CSD.

HONOR BOOKS

From the beginning of the awarding of the medals, committees could, and usually did, cite other books as worthy of attention. Such books were referred to as runners-up. In 1971 the term "runners-up," used to designate books cited with the annual Newbery and Caldecott Medal winners, was changed to "honor books." The new terminology was made retroactive so that all runners-up are now referred to as Newbery or Caldecott Honor Books.

At the same meeting, the Board of Directors of the Children's Services Division approved silver facsimile seals with the designation "Newbery Honor Book" and "Caldecott Honor Book," which may be placed on the honor books in similar fashion to the use made of the gold facsimile seals of the medals placed on the award-winning books. The gold and silver facsimile seals are sold by the Association for Library Service to Children, with all profits going to support the division's programs, including the

Frederic G. Melcher Scholarship Fund. Permission for photographic reproduction of the medals is also controlled by the association; profits from commercial reproduction also go to the Scholarship Fund.

In 1978 the ALSC board approved the presentation of certificates to the authors of the Newbery Honor Books and the illustrators of the Caldecott Honor Books. Certificates were presented for the first time in 1986.

Although some procedures have changed over the years the awards have been given, and some rules or aspects of what the awards are for have been clarified or modified, the basic purpose of honoring distinguished American children's books has not changed. Numerous committees have studied virtually every aspect of the award-giving procedure, the rationale, and the impact of the awards over the years. Such study is likely to continue and ensures a vital life to these awards that have had such an impact on the quality of American literature for children.

John Newbery: Bookseller, Entrepreneur, and Advocate for Children's Literature

Ronald G. Edwards

John Newbery was one of the most influential businessmen and booksellers in England in the eighteenth century, but, interestingly enough, very little has been written about this extraordinary individual. Only one biography, *A Bookseller of the Last Century*, by Charles Welsh, documents his life from start to finish.[1] Similarly, very few letters, journals, and articles exist that accurately portray Newbery's accomplishments. Still, today he is considered a pivotal figure in the development of children's books. Known as the founder of modern publishing for children, his legacy lives on to this day. Since 1922, when Frederic Melcher awarded the first Newbery Medal, John Newbery has been commemorated. Presented each year by the American Library Association for the best-written children's book of the preceding year, the Newbery Medal remains a testimony to Newbery's place in the field of children's literature.

Born at Waltham St. Lawrence, Berkshire, in 1713, John Newbery grew up surrounded by cornfields and the lush, green countryside of the Thames valley. As a result of his modest socioeconomic position, his education was kept to a minimum. For the most part, he was a self-educated man who read anything he could get his hands on. The lack of formal schooling he received was somewhat compensated for by his voracious appetite for reading books, as well as his intense work ethic, instilled in him by his father. His profound love of learning played a major role in his

Reprinted from *Journal of Youth Services in Libraries* 10 (Fall 1996): 58–64. Ronald G. Edwards is the head of the Curriculum Resource Center, Jerome Library, Bowling Green (Ohio) State University.

success throughout his life, both as an astute businessman and as a benefactor to aspiring writers. Newbery's emphasis on the importance of acquiring knowledge is manifested in many of the books he eventually published.[2] Certainly, it is evident in the way he conducted his business affairs throughout his successful career.

EARLY YEARS

John Newbery gave up his agricultural lifestyle at the relatively young age of sixteen to become an assistant to William Carnan, a printer from Reading. Carnan was the editor of the *Reading Mercury*, one of the earliest provincial newspapers in England. Although Carnan's business was primarily that of publishing a newspaper, he was also involved in other business ventures such as books, cutlery, and haberdashery.[3] More than likely, it was this exploration into other facets of the business arena that may have inspired Newbery later on in his career.

Newbery's association with William Carnan lasted from 1729 to 1737. In 1737, Carnan died, leaving a portion of his business to Newbery. As fate would have it, Newbery fell in love with and married Carnan's widow, automatically becoming stepfather to her three children by William Carnan. In addition, Newbery had three more children of his own by this marriage.

From the very beginning of his career, it was obvious that John Newbery would be successful regarding his own business enterprises. He was the consummate professional, an attribute acquired during his formative years at Waltham St. Lawrence. His concern for detail and keen sense of the business market were exemplified in everything he undertook. Charles Welsh vividly portrays Newbery's attitude in his biographical work from 1885.

> He seems to have bought or noted the prices of anything and everything he thought he could sell. . . . Wherever he went his mind appears to have been constantly on his business.[4]

Newbery ran the business in Reading for a number of years after Carnan's death and did so very effectively. Although Reading was considered an important city regarding the selling of grain and other commodities, it was not a pivotal location for the mercantile business. Newbery felt that if he were going to really achieve the success he longed for and knew he could attain, he would have to expand his business beyond the boundaries of this part of England.

CHILDREN'S BOOKS

Newbery decided to relocate his business interests to London in 1743. By this time, he had begun to diversify his business ventures as well as expand his book-publishing and printing enterprises. Although he had been involved in the publishing of books in Reading, Newbery started to tread on completely new ground in London with the publication of children's books. A few other books for children had recently been produced, but for the most part, this area of the publishing industry was still quite new and unexplored territory. Thomas Boreman had distributed a set of ten miniature books called the *Gigantic Histories* between 1740 and 1743. Likewise, Mary Cooper had published *The Child's New Plaything* in 1742, while Benjamin Collins had issued the first edition of *A Pretty Book for Children* in 1743.[5] These offerings represented only a few isolated cases, though they really did not reflect the dearth of information that existed for children.

Newbery firmly believed that there was a growing market for and interest in the publication of books specifically designed for and read by children of all ages. Society was changing its attitudes about the education of children, and Newbery recognized this slowly moving social revolution. A freer mindset toward children was gradually surfacing. Before this time, society has been clearly divided between the aristocracy and the peasantry. With the coming of the Industrial Revolution and the emergence of the middle class, a completely different social structure began to appear. The concept of childhood, which had not existed before 1700, now took on its own identity. The discovery of childhood as a distinct phase of life, apart from adolescence, started to evolve. The middle class began to shape societal values as well as the social institutions that were being constructed.

This changing social climate prompted the need for a new body of literature. The literature not only needed to echo and support these changing class values and beliefs, but also had to answer the need for instructional materials by which children could develop the social skills necessary to survive in this evolving social milieu.

Newbery clearly understood the growing economic significance of children in the overall scheme of the book market.[6] He sold many of his books to the aristocracy, but he relied on this segment of the population primarily for their patronage more than anything else.[7] It was the middle class, though, that Newbery focused his attention on and that really accounted for his success in children's publishing. By exploiting the emerging middle classes, who were eager to achieve their newly discovered role in society and who wanted the best for their children, Newbery found his own niche in the publishing field.[8] This exploitation was not something done just for the sake of monetary gain. Newbery knew too well that unless he was proactive and consistent regarding the publishing of children's books, the upward trend he created in children's book publishing could easily come to a dramatic halt. Darton comments on Newbery's attitude concerning the infiltration of the market in his book *Children's Books in England,* from which the following remark is taken: "He grasped one great permanent truth of the publishing trade—that invasion of the market must be constant and continuous."[9]

In comparing the number of juvenile books that Newbery published with that of other publishers, it is apparent that he was right on track concerning the necessity to publish as many books as possible. Newbery did not want the general public to lose its appetite for children's books. Although not all of the books were written and published with the young reader in mind, Newbery was able to produce over fifty new books during the last twenty-three years of his life. This accomplishment was not only a tribute to his persistence in the publishing field but also a reflection of his business acumen. The fact that most of his other businesses thrived during this period is additional testimony to his prowess as a businessman.

OTHER VENTURES

Newbery's commitment to providing educational material for children did not stop with children's literature. He was also involved with the manufacture of games that taught children to read, write, and spell. As with other methods he employed in the advertising and marketing of children's books, Newbery packaged some of these games in the selling of his many publications. Not all of the games he produced were strictly for educational reasons. Some were manufactured for the amusement of the child.

By far one of Newbery's most unique creations was his publication of *The Lilliputian Magazine,* a periodical devoted entirely to children. This innovative business venture was a first for any publisher up to the mid-eighteenth century.[10] Produced in 1751–52, Newbery intended to publish it as an ongoing project. Unfortunately, it did not meet with the success he meant for it to have. Instead, the publication ended up to be a composite volume rather than a regularly published journal.[11] Even though it had exhibited all of the quality ingredients that his other publications contained, this short-lived magazine turned out to be one of the few disappointments experienced by Newbery. Some critics maintain that it was the forerunner of the nineteenth-century version of children's comics.[12]

PUBLISHING INNOVATIONS

John Newbery's devotion to producing excellent products knew no boundaries. He constantly sought to achieve quality in everything he manufactured and sold. Besides improving the basic format of the books he published, Newbery set standards, not only in the details of the books he published but also in the actual engravings used in the material.[13] He was the first major publisher to emphasize the notion of the illustrated book for children.[14] At every turn, he tried to employ skilled artists to write and illustrate his books, a feature not prevalent in the business before Newbery began utilizing this method. In the same manner, he used the highest quality paper and inks available. The binding techniques employed by his firm were truly innovative and superior to many of his competitors. Instead of using leather in his binding process, he bound many of his publications in the vellum manner, a much cheaper and longer-lasting method.

PATRON OF THE ARTIST

Most of the accolades Newbery received were for his numerous publications of children's books. He contributed significantly in the areas of periodicals and adult books as well. Shortly after he arrived in London, Newbery became associated with a number of literary figures in England. Among these individuals were Oliver Goldsmith, Christopher Smart, Tobias Smollett, and Samuel Johnson. Smollett proved to be very instrumental regarding the periodicals' side of the business, editing *The British Magazine*. Smart and Johnson were involved in writing books for the adult audience.

But it was Oliver Goldsmith who was the most prominent figure in the entire group. During his employment with Newbery, Goldsmith published numerous books, including *Citizen of the World* and *The Vicar of Wakefield*. In fact, it is in *The Vicar of Wakefield* that Goldsmith paints a very complimentary portrait of the publisher by referring to Newbery as "the philanthropic bookseller of St. Paul's Churchyard."[15] Goldsmith also assisted with the children's side of Newbery's publishing firm by writing *An History of England in a Series of Letters from a Nobleman to His Son*, published in 1764. Some people believe that it may have been Goldsmith who wrote *Goody Two-Shoes*, but this is speculative at best.[16] One fact that cannot be refuted, though, is Newbery's assistance to Goldsmith, serving as his employer and patron for part of his career.

REASONS FOR NEWBERY'S SUCCESS

Many reasons exist for the success achieved by John Newbery as a bookseller and publisher. Some individuals attribute his achievements to being in the right place at the right time in history. Others maintain that it was because society was changing and that these evolving social conditions enhanced his chances for a successful business career. Both of these explanations are definitely valid and on target. Each reason certainly impacted the outcome of his individual accomplishments. More than likely, though, it was Newbery's basic character and his upbringing that were largely responsible for his overall level of success. The following comment from Welsh's book on Newbery sums it up very succinctly:

> If he had not worked hard at his books while at home at Waltham, he would never have qualified himself to succeed to the business of Carnan, and thus to lay the foundation of its success.[17]

This basic philosophy remained consistent throughout Newbery's life. It is impossible to say for sure where Newbery acquired his unique blend of common sense and business savvy, or his tenacious appetite for perfection in his work. Some of these attributes were probably nurtured during the years he spent as an apprentice in Reading at the *Reading Mercury*. His zeal for the publishing of children's books is evident. Unlike many of his competitors, Newbery realized that if publishing was going to survive, he would have to convince the public, especially the middle class, that there was a need for quality material. To accomplish this task, he utilized his own newspapers to advertise the books he produced. An ingenious advertiser, Newbery knew that effective advertising was the key to selling books or anything else. His art of "puffing" his products was unrivaled.[18] William Noblett maintains that Newbery's marketing techniques were far ahead of his time and extremely sophisticated for the eighteenth century.[19]

Another ploy that Newbery utilized was to advertise his books, as well as the other products he sold, in his own publications. He would often refer to these items in the actual text of his children's books. His reference to Dr. James's Fever Powder in *Goody Two-Shoes* is a perfect example of this method.[20]

Although the impact that John Locke had on Newbery was more peripheral than other factors, this aspect cannot be ignored or underestimated. A so-called disciple of Locke, Newbery believed that reading had a great influence regarding the child-development process.[21] Since the predominant view in England during the eighteenth century was that books should inculcate some moral, while reflecting society's values, Newbery did his part by publishing children's books with these basic ideas in mind.[22] His first published book, *A Pretty Pocket-Book*, adheres to this belief. In much the same way that Locke had organized his own theories of teaching and learning, Newbery formulated his beliefs. Newbery recognized the importance of maintaining agreeable surroundings as an effective incentive for teaching the child. Although education was to be taken seriously, it was not supposed to be a burden. Newbery wanted his games to be used for instructional purposes, but he also attempted to make these products as inviting and enjoyable as possible.[23]

CONCLUSION

In the final analysis, what was it that made John Newbery stand apart from and above his contemporaries and predecessors? Commitment! Newbery possessed the courage to take chances and exhibited the willingness to publish material for children. In this respect, he was the first publisher to make a concerted effort to do so.[24] He knew that the only way to achieve his lofty goals was by convincing the general public of the need for books. Newbery may not have published any books that have stood the test of time, but he alone was responsible for infiltrating the book market. He made people aware of the importance of children's books for both educational purposes and enjoyment. Because of his undying commitment to children's books, John Newbery will be remembered forever by educators throughout the world.

REFERENCES

1. Charles Welsh, *A Bookseller of the Last Century: Being Some Account of the Life of John Newbery and of the Books He Published with a Notice of the Later Newberys* (1885; reprint, Clifton, N.J.: Augustus M. Kelley, 1972).
2. Mary F. Thwaite, "John Newbery: Two Centuries After," *Horn Book* 44 (April 1968): 157.
3. F. J. Harvey Darton, *Children's Books in England: Five Centuries of Social Life*, 3d ed. (Cambridge: Cambridge Univ. Pr., 1982), 120.
4. Welsh, *A Bookseller*, 13.
5. Margaret Kinnell, "Publishing for Children: 1700–1780," in *Children's Literature: An Illustrated History* (Oxford: Oxford Univ. Pr., 1995), 26-45.
6. Ibid., 35.
7. William Noblett, "John Newbery: Publisher Extraordinary," *History Today* 22 (April 1972): 270.

8. Ibid.
9. Darton, *Children's Books in England*, 135.
10. Noblett, "John Newbery," 269.
11. Kinnell, "Publishing for Children," 37.
12. Noblett, "John Newbery," 269
13. Darton, *Children's Books in England*, 136.
14. Ibid.
15. Thwaite, "John Newbery," 161.
16. Darton, *Children's Books in England*, 122.
17. Welsh, *A Bookseller*, 80.
18. Ibid., 106.
19. Noblett, "John Newbery," 268.
20. Ibid.
21. Humphrey Carpenter and Mari Prichard, *The Oxford Companion to Children's Literature* (Oxford: Oxford Univ. Pr., 1984), 375.
22. Alec Ellis, *A History of Children's Reading and Literature* (Oxford: Pergamon, 1968), 5.
23. Noblett. "John Newbery," 266.
24. Ellis, *A History of Children's Reading*, 3.

The Newbery Awards

1999–1922

1999 NEWBERY AWARD

Holes

Louis Sachar
Frances Foster Books/Farrar Straus Giroux

Louis Sachar

Stanley Yelnats, the heir to his family's curse of bad luck, is convicted of a crime he didn't commit. He serves his sentence at Camp Green Lake, a dry, flat wasteland where the warden assigns each inmate the task of digging one deep hole every day. Hole by hole, Stanley and his friend Zero dig their destiny.

Holes is masterfully unified in character, setting, and theme. As timeless and outrageously funny as a tall tale, *Holes* ultimately charts the heroic journey of two very real boys.

1999 HONOR BOOK

A Long Way from Chicago

Richard Peck   Dial Books for Young Readers

Joey recounts his annual summer trips to rural Illinois with his sister Mary Alice during the Great Depression to visit their extraordinary grandmother. Richard Peck has created a memorable world filled with characters who are larger than life and twice as entertaining.

1998 Awards

Out of the Dust
Karen Hesse   Scholastic

Fourteen-year-old Billie Jo relates how her mother dies after an accident with burning kerosene. Blaming both herself and her father, she is unable to express herself through her piano playing because of the burns that scar her hands. She leaves but quickly returns to her home "of dust" and she realizes how much a part of her it is.

HONORS

Ella Enchanted.   Gail Carson Levine.   HarperCollins.

Spunky, stubborn, and very clever, this new Cinderella spends a lifetime trying to outwit the curse of a fairy's unwelcome gift of obedience. In a kingdom populated with ogres, giants, princes, and fairies, Ella begins a fruitless quest to have the curse lifted, only to discover that she has that power within herself.

Lily's Crossing.   Patricia Reilly Giff.   Delacorte.

During her 1944 summer vacation in the Rockaways, ten-year-old Lily's best friend moves away and her beloved father Poppy goes off to war. Then Lily meets Albert, a young Hungarian refugee with whom she builds a poignant friendship based on shared loneliness, secrets, and lies.

Wringer.   Jerry Spinelli.   HarperCollins.

Palmer LaRue dreads his approaching birthday because he does not want to be a wringer, one of the ten-year-old boys who breaks the necks of pigeons wounded at the town's pigeon shoot fund-raiser. When his three bullying friends suspect he is sheltering a stray pigeon, Palmer decides to take a personal stand against this annual rite of passage.

1997 Awards

The View from Saturday
E. L. Konigsburg   Jean Karl/Atheneum

Mrs. Olinski selects four of her sixth-grade students to be the Academic Bowl team. No one understands her choice of these particular students, including Mrs. Olinski, who continues to question herself. The students surprise everyone with their unique contributions to the challenges of competition.

HONORS

A Girl Named Disaster.   Nancy Farmer.   Jackson/Orchard.

When Nhamo (Disaster) flees her village to search for her father in Zimbabwe, she is lost on Lake Cabora Bassa in Mozambique. Alone, she survives harsh weather, wild animals, and near starvation before building a new life in the world of her father's people.

Moorchild.   Eloise McGraw.   Margaret K. McElderry/Simon & Schuster.

Moorchild Moql becomes the changeling Saaski, half-human, half-Folk, and an outcast in both worlds. The reader is drawn into the lives of the moorfolk who fear Saaski and those who try to understand her and support her.

The Thief.   Megan Whalen Turner.   Greenwillow.

Freed from the royal dungeons and commanded to steal an ancient talisman from supernatural guardians, young Gen pulls off an astonishing scam and in the process rescues his own country from a threatened invasion.

Belle Prater's Boy.   Ruth White.   Farrar Straus Giroux.

Gypsy's cousin Woodrow comes to live next door, bringing with him a mystery and the key to a secret that Gypsy keeps from herself. Grandparents and Gypsy's supportive mother and stepfather create a loving environment in which the children can come to grips with their losses.

--------------------- **1996 Award** ---------------------

The Midwife's Apprentice
Karen Cushman   Clarion

The central character, Brat, is a homeless waif who first appears sleeping in a dung heap "unwashed, unnourished, unloved, and unlovely . . . ." From a person with no hopes, no dreams, and no expectations she becomes the midwife's apprentice—a person with a name and a place in the world. An excellent portrayal of medieval England.

HONORS

What Jamie Saw.   Carolyn Coman.   Front Street.

What Jamie Saw is a gripping interior novel that portrays a desperate mother and her quietly heroic son as they move from an impossibly bleak situation toward a promise of hope. Coman captures Jamie's fear, his uncertainty, and his confusion as well as his growing confidence and ability to stand up for himself.

The Watsons Go to Birmingham—1963.   Christopher Paul Curtis.   Delacorte.

From its hilarious opening chapters to its shattering conclusion, *The Watsons Go to Birmingham* is a compelling novel that brings to life an African-American family. It draws together everyday events in such a way as to send the Watsons on a journey to Birmingham that will change them forever. The depiction of devastating events in Birmingham integrates the dichotomy of familial love and stability with the racial strife of the 1960s.

Yolonda's Genius. Carol Fenner. Margaret K. McElderry/Simon & Schuster.
Fenner portrays memorable characters and a vivid, authentic place in this engaging story of a bright, feisty fifth grader. Yolonda is determined to bring to light her younger brother's extraordinary talent of transforming the world around him into the music he makes.

The Great Fire. Jim Murphy. Scholastic.
The riveting narrative of the 1871 Chicago fire thrusts the reader into the center of the raging conflagration. Murphy weaves eyewitness accounts of the disaster with factual and social commentary, period photographs, etchings, and maps into memorable nonfiction writing.

1995 Award

Walk Two Moons
Sharon Creech   HarperCollins

Thirteen-year-old Salamanca Tree Hiddle sets out on a cross-country journey with her grandparents to see her mother, who has not returned from a visit to Idaho. Sal entertains her grandparents by telling them about her new friend Phoebe, and in so doing begins to understand herself and her own mother. The book, packed with humor and affection, is an odyssey of unexpected twists and surprising conclusions.

HONORS

Catherine, Called Birdy. Karen Cushman. Clarion.
In the course of her fourteenth year, Catherine keeps a journal of her perceptive observations and longings for adventure and independence. Her lively, humorous descriptions of life on a thirteenth century English manor, midst unwanted suitors and ever-present fleas, reach through to time to speak to modern readers.

The Ear, the Eye, and the Arm. Nancy Farmer. Jackson/Orchard.
A kidnapping of the General's three children in twenty-second-century Zimbabwe sets off a dramatic chase. In a series of extraordinary adventures, the children play a crucial role in a thrilling battle against the forces of evil. This futuristic detective story is interwoven with African's history, present-day concerns, and a variety of colorful characters.

1994 Award

The Giver
Lois Lowry   Houghton

Twelve-year-old Jonas performs well in the impressively ordered society that the Elders have developed. But when he is selected to be the new "Receiver," Jonas begins to unravel the truth that underlies his world.

HONORS

Crazy Lady. Jane Leslie Conly. HarperCollins.

Twelve-year-old Vernon's initially reluctant, off-beat friendship with an alcoholic and her developmentally disabled son has repercussions throughout the neighborhood, changing the lives of all involved. The reader becomes aware that Vernon's growing self-esteem and maturity come about through his commitment to helping his friends.

Eleanor Roosevelt: A Life of Discovery. Russell Freedman. Clarion Books.

Through compelling text and contemporary photographs, Eleanor Roosevelt is shown moving from a sheltered, unhappy childhood to the world's stage. This fascinating biography of a remarkable and complex woman is meticulously researched.

Dragon's Gate. Laurence Yep. HarperCollins.

Dragon's Gate is a carefully researched, well-written account of the lives of the Chinese who built the transcontinental railroad in the Sierra Mountains. This glimpse into the complex working community of California at the time of the Civil War is also a sensitive portrayal of the relationship between a father and son.

1993 Award

Missing May
Cynthia Rylant   Jackson/Orchard

Twelve-year-old Summer lives with her Aunt May and Uncle Ob in the mountains of West Virginia. When May dies, Summer, Uncle Ob, and Summer's friend, Cletus, try to get her back—or at least to get word of her—and to alleviate the pain. This trio of lovingly described characters journeys from intense grief to the understanding that love is never truly lost.

HONORS

What Hearts. Bruce Brooks. A Laura Geringer Book, a HarperCollins imprint.

Seven-year-old Asa, by far the best in his class, comes home from the last day of school with a knapsack full of prizes to find that his whole world has changed. Asa tries to make sense of a world in which he is challenged and put down by a domineering stepfather and only partially sustained by his loving but disturbed mother. Four stories show Asa at seven, nine, eleven, and twelve, struggling to find the secret of connection with others.

The Dark-thirty: Southern Tales of the Supernatural. Patricia C. McKissack. Knopf.

The dark-thirty is that special half hour of twilight, just before dark, when everyone hurries home because the spirits and monsters come out. This collection of spine-tingling tales ranges from the time of slavery to the civil rights movement. Strong characterization, classic themes, and suspenseful plots are strongly crafted in the oral tradition of African-American folklore.

Somewhere in the Darkness. Walter Dean Myers. Scholastic Hardcover.

Jimmy Little had always wanted a father. However, when Crab, his father, who is virtually a stranger, appears in a dark hallway straight from a prison hospital, it is not at all what he had hoped for. On the tense, frightening trip with Crab to Chicago and then to Alabama, Jimmy finds he must learn self-knowledge as well as compassion to deal with a difficult and dangerous situation.

1992 Award

Shiloh
Phyllis Reynolds Naylor   Atheneum

Marty Preston, an eleven-year-old West Virginian boy, befriends a stray dog and while protecting the dog from abuse wrestles with universal questions of honesty, commitment, and ethical decision making. Marty discovers that discerning right from wrong is not as straightforward as he had imagined.

HONORS

Nothing But the Truth: A Documentary Novel. Avi. Jackson/Orchard.

Avi's documentary approach chronicles the results of a teacher's objection to a ninth grader's humming along with "The Star Spangled Banner." School rules stipulate that students are to stand at "respectful, silent attention." Miscommunication, misperceptions, and personal viewpoints of right, wrong, and protected freedoms propel the characters rapidly into a crisis situation that forces the reader to explore issues of perception, reality, bias, and expediency.

The Wright Brothers: How They Invented the Airplane. Russell Freedman. Holiday House.

In a spirited blend of science, history, and biography, Freedman presents a fascinating portrait of a new age. Using Wilber and Orville Wright's own photographs as well as excerpts from their notes and journals, he creates a uniquely personal and engaging view of their accomplishments.

1991 Award

Maniac Magee
Jerry Spinelli   Little, Brown

Jeffrey Lionel Magee is a legendary character who runs the rails faster than other kids run the ground. Jeffrey bunts "the world's first frogball for a four-bagger" and performs other amazing feats.

HONOR

The True Confessions of Charlotte Doyle. Avi. Jackson/Orchard.

Avi weaves a finely crafted tale of high seas adventure and gripping suspense, made rich by thirteen-year-old Charlotte's deepening understanding of honor and herself.

1990 Award

Number the Stars
Lois Lowry   Houghton

When ten-year-old Annemarie Johansen's family decides to pretend that her friend Ellen Rosen is her sister, they become involved in the effort to save the Danish Jews from the Nazis. As the author deftly portrays deep friendship, a strong family, and heroism in wartime, the story builds to a tense climax.

HONORS

Afternoon of the Elves. Janet Taylor Lisle. Jackson/Orchard.

Fascinated by Sarah-Kate's backyard elf village, Hillary is unprepared for the secret side of the older girl's life. Strong, tough, an outcast at school, Sarah-Kate has been doing whatever she must to care for herself and her mentally ill mother. When her plight is discovered by adults, disturbing but necessary changes occur.

The Winter Room. Gary Paulsen. Jackson/Orchard.

From the first page to the last, this story of farm life in northern Minnesota is so engrossing that the place and the people seem real. Eldon, the eleven-year-old narrator, takes the reader through the seasons and into the winter room, where stories are "not for believing so much, as to be believed in."

Shabanu, Daughter of the Wind. Suzanne Fisher Staples. Knopf.

Spirited and courageous Shabanu, younger daughter of present-day Pakistani camel herders, loves her family's life and her role in caring for their camels. Both Shabanu and her older sister are betrothed to brothers, but as her sister's wedding nears, a calamity occurs that changes forever the life of independent Shabanu.

1989 Award

Joyful Noise: Poems for Two Voices
Paul Fleischman
Illustrated by Eric Beddows   Zolotow/Harper

Fourteen poems, using two voices, sometimes alternating, sometimes together, offer listeners a look at what insects just might think of themselves and their world. The book lice, grasshoppers, house crickets, and their poetic companions are illustrated in soft yet often comical black-and-white pencil drawings.

HONORS

In the Beginning: Creation Stories from Around the World. Virginia Hamilton. Illustrated by Barry Moser. Harcourt.

Stories from African, Chinese, Native American, and Guinean peoples are represented among the twenty-five creation myths found in this collection. Faithfully retold, the stories are followed by notes about their sources. Dramatic watercolor paintings accent each tale.

Scorpions. Walter Dean Myers. Harper.

Hoping to find a way to raise money for an appeal for his imprisoned older brother, twelve-year-old Jamal agrees to try to become the leader of his brother's Harlem gang, the Scorpions. Involvement with the gang (and the gun he is given) leads to tragedy for Jamal and his friend Tito.

1988 Award

Lincoln: A Photobiography
Russell Freedman   Clarion

An ambitious man, Lincoln struggled hard to get an education, to build his law practice, and to become politically successful. The man, his wit, and his wisdom are vividly and honestly portrayed in this straightforward biography and its ninety photographs.

HONORS

After the Rain. Norma Fox Mazer. Morrow.

Fifteen-year-old Rachel tries to balance her concern for her own life with her grandfather's need for her help. Never close to the old man, she slowly comes to love him. As she struggles to help him maintain his independence, he weakens and nears death.

Hatchet. Gary Paulsen. Bradbury.

When the pilot dies of a heart attack, Brian crash-lands the small plane in the Canadian wilderness. Left with only a hatchet and the clothes he is wearing, Brian begins a gripping fifty-four-day ordeal that challenges his physical and psychological skills to their limits.

1987 Award

The Whipping Boy   Sid Fleischman
Illustrated by Peter Sís   Greenwillow

Whenever Prince Brat does anything bad, Jemmy, his whipping boy, is punished. The spoiled prince decides to run away from the palace, forcing

Jemmy to go with him. Far from the safety of the court, the prince quickly learns how little he knows about the outside world and how important Jemmy is to his survival.

HONORS

On My Honor. Marion Dane Bauer. Clarion.

Before leaving on a bike ride with his impetuous friend Tony, Joel gives his father his word of honor that he will not swim in a river known to be dangerous. Tony convinces Joel that the river is safe; the two swim; and Tony drowns. Joel is left alone to face his guilt, both sets of parents, and his own grief.

Volcano: The Eruption and Healing of Mount St. Helens. Patricia Lauber. Bradbury.

The eruption of Mount St. Helens and the subsequent regrowth of plants are vividly portrayed in color photographs and a dynamic text. The volcanic eruption is seen not as just a disaster, but as a builder of life on this planet.

A Fine White Dust. Cynthia Rylant. Bradbury.

Although neither his parents nor his best friend are particularly religious, Peter feels a need for something deeper than just churchgoing. When an itinerant preacher comes to town, Peter is mesmerized by the man and "saved." Invited to go away with the preacher, Peter reluctantly agrees, only to be left behind and forgotten.

1986 Award

Sarah Plain and Tall
Patricia MacLachlan   Zolotow/Harper

Life on the prairie with two children and no wife is lonely and difficult, so Caleb and Anna's father advertises for a wife. Sarah answers his ad and soon agrees to come all the way from Maine for a visit. Captivated by her, Anna and Caleb worry that Sarah misses the sea too much to stay with them.

HONORS

Commodore Perry in the Land of the Shogun. Rhoda Blumberg. Lothrop.

Commodore Perry's fascinating mission to Japan in 1853 is told at a lively pace, with special attention given to the negotiating skill that led to his success; to his sensitivity to cultural differences; and to his just plain curiosity. The accompanying pictures include many sketched by the Japanese and the Americans who were with Matthew Perry.

Dogsong. Gary Paulsen. Bradbury.

Unhappy with the snowmobile-and-television society that seems to have taken over his Eskimo village, Russell turns to Oogruk, the old man of the village, for help in finding a path back to the old ways. With Oogruk's advice and encouragement, Russell begins an arduous dogsled journey northward to find his own "song."

1985 Award

The Hero and the Crown
Robin McKinley   Greenwillow

The daughter of the king of Damar and his second wife (a witch woman from the north), Aerin does not fit in at court. Unable to succeed her father to the throne, she must instead find her own destiny. Wielding her blue sword, she not only defeats dragons but finally becomes the hero of the kingdom.

HONORS

The Moves Make the Man. Bruce Brooks. Harper.

The first black to go to the formerly all-white junior high school, Jerome is a passionate basketball player. When he meets Bix Rivers, an unstable outsider who is a gifted athlete, Jerome decides to teach him basketball. As they play the game, Bix's mental illness becomes more apparent, and Jerome is less able to help him.

One-Eyed Cat. Paula Fox. Bradbury.

After his minister father takes his new air rifle away from him and puts it in the attic, Ned sneaks upstairs, takes it, fires it once, and is terrified that he may have hit a cat. Struggling with his guilt, he tells one lie after another until he cannot bear it anymore and must confess to someone.

Like Jake and Me. Mavis Jukes. Illustrated by Lloyd Bloom. Knopf.

Alex wants to be liked by his rugged cowboy stepfather, but there are still barriers between the two. When Alex notices a wolf spider on Jake's neck and calmly mentions it, the rugged cowboy totally panics, admitting his terror of spiders. Alex comes to the rescue, and the two finally come to appreciate each other and their differences.

1984 Award

Dear Mr. Henshaw   Beverly Cleary
Illustrated by Paul O. Zelinsky   Morrow

Leigh Botts starts writing to the author of *Ways to Amuse a Dog* in second grade. Year after year the letters, and then a diary, become vehicles for expressing his feelings about himself, his parents' divorce, and his problems in school. Leigh's growth and acceptance of the divorce are tempered with much humor.

HONORS

The Wish Giver: Three Tales of Coven Tree. Bill Brittain. Illustrated by
Andrew Glass. Harper.

Thaddeus Blinn, the wish giver, sells Polly, Rowena, Henry, and Stew Meat
wishes. All they have to do is hold the white card with the dot and wish carefully. The first three make their wishes with dire but comical consequences
and leave Stew Meat to use his to undo everything they have done.

Sugaring Time. Kathryn Lasky. Photographs by Christopher G.
Knight. Macmillan.

The author and photographer record a family's old-fashioned method of
sugaring. When the right time finally comes, family members tap the maple
trees, boil the sap, and enjoy a sugar-on-snow party and a pancake breakfast.
The family's enjoyment of sugaring is evident in the often poetic text and the
clear black-and-white photographs.

The Sign of the Beaver. Elizabeth George Speare. Houghton.

Left alone in the Maine wilderness, Matt first loses his rifle and food and then
is savagely stung by bees. Found by Saknis, chief of the Beaver tribe, Matt is
cared for in exchange for teaching the chief's grandson to read. As the boys'
friendship develops, Matt gains an appreciation for the heritage and skills of
the Beaver tribe.

A Solitary Blue. Cynthia Voigt. Atheneum.

Abandoned at the age of seven by his cause-conscious mother, Jeff is left to
fend for himself and take care of his absent-minded-professor father. Not until Jeff is stricken with pneumonia at the age of twelve does his father understand how he, too, has deserted his son. Slowly the two build a close, strong
relationship that is able to help them survive and grow.

1983 Award

Dicey's Song
Cynthia Voigt   Atheneum

Finally settled in with Gram Tillerman while their mother is in a mental
hospital, Dicey and her brothers and sisters discover that it is not easy to become a family. They must learn to love and trust Gram—and she
them—while they try to adjust to a new school and make friends.

HONORS

Graven Images. Paul Fleischman. Illustrated by Andrew Glass. Harper.

Three gripping stories, two sinister and one funny and all with historical settings, are centered on graven images: a wooden boy with a frightening secret,
a weathervane that leads to true love, and a statue ordered by a ghost.

Homesick: My Own Story. Jean Fritz. Illustrated by Margot Tomes. Putnam.

Fritz remembers with humor and poignancy two years of her childhood in China during the turbulent 1920s. She contends with being a "foreign devil," losing a longed-for baby sister, and, most of all, longing for the United States, a country she has never seen.

Sweet Whispers, Brother Rush. Virginia Hamilton. Philomel.

Life changes radically for fourteen-year-old Tree and her older retarded brother when the ghost of Brother Rush appears to Tree, first in the street and then in her home. The handsome ghost of her mother's brother takes her back in time to bear witness to the past and to learn about the terrible disease that is killing her own brother.

The Blue Sword. Robin McKinley. Greenwillow.

Angharad Crewe is yanked out of an easy life on a Homelander outpost and thrust into one of rigorous training for her prophesied role as deliverer of the Hillfolk. She earns the right to carry the Blue Sword into battle, and with it she heroically leads a small band of warriors against the nonhuman Northerners.

Doctor De Soto. William Steig. Farrar.

As mice dentists, the diminutive De Sotos have always refused to treat dangerous animals until a miserable fox appears begging for help. The compassionate mice cleverly find a way to rid the fox of his pain while guaranteeing their own safety.

1982 Award

A Visit to William Blake's Inn: Poems for Innocent and Experienced Travelers Nancy Willard
Illustrated by Alice and Martin Provensen Harcourt

Written in the spirit of William Blake, these magical poems are built around the visit of a child to Blake's inn. It is staffed by mighty dragons that brew and bake, angels that wash feather beds, and animals that dance to the music of the Marmalade Man.

HONORS

Ramona Quimby, Age 8. Beverly Cleary. Illustrated by Alan Tiegreen. Morrow.

Ramona is now starting the third grade and her life is full of the usual hilarious trials that cause her to be labeled a "nuisance and show-off" by her new teacher. Whether she is deciding she prefers her printed Q to the floppy cursive one, getting raw egg in her hair, or facing an interminably boring Sunday, Ramona is always a memorable character.

Upon the Head of the Goat: A Childhood in Hungary 1939–1944.
Aranka Siegal. Farrar.

The destruction of nine-year-old Piri's family begins with Hungary's occupation by the Nazis. Her mother valiantly tries to keep the family together and safe, but one loss after another occurs until they board trains that will take them to Auschwitz. Siegal's book is a powerful autobiography.

1981 Award

Jacob Have I Loved
Katherine Paterson   Crowell

Although she takes pride in her twin sister's singing talent, Wheeze (Louise) is jealous of the attention Caroline gets on their Chesapeake Bay island. It is only when she leaves and starts a life as a midwife in Kentucky that Wheeze comes to understand that she has always been loved and accepted for herself.

HONORS

The Fledgling.   Jane Langton.   Illustrated by Erik Blegvad.   Harper.

Frail young Georgie, almost light enough to blow away, is obsessed with her belief that she can fly. When a large Canada goose she has befriended hoots outside her window, Georgie hops on his back and flies away. Night after night they soar above Walden Pond until one misfortune and then another end Georgie's flying forever.

A Ring of Endless Light.   Madeleine L'Engle.   Farrar.

Sixteen-year-old Vicky and her family spend the summer on a New England island with her dying grandfather. All summer long she and her family are preoccupied with the mysteries of life, death, and eternity, yet there is still time for Vicky to help with a Marine Biology Station dolphin project and to date two boys.

1980 Award

A Gathering of Days: A New England Girl's Journal, 1830–1832
Joan W. Blos   Scribner

Catherine Cabot Hall sporadically writes in her journal, filling it with recipes, excerpts from her copy book, secrets, fears, confidences, details of her adjustment to her stepmother, and thoughts on the pain of a friend's death. Though fiction, the journal is believable, and Catherine is easy to like.

HONOR

The Road from Home: The Story of an Armenian Girl.   David Kherdian. Greenwillow.

After the Turks finish with their slaughter of nearly two million Armenians, Veron is the only survivor of her immediate family. When the Greeks attack Turkey, Veron and her aunt and cousin escape to Greece, and from there she travels to the United States, a mail-order bride and the future mother of the author.

1979 Award

The Westing Game
Ellen Raskin   Dutton

An expensive apartment building mysteriously fills up with sixteen occupants—all named as heirs or possible murderers in millionaire Sam Westing's will. The sixteen are paired, given $10,000, and challenged to discover who really killed Sam Westing.

HONOR

The Great Gilly Hopkins. Katherine Paterson. Crowell.

Abandoned as a preschooler, Gilly has gone through a succession of foster homes. Smart, self-sufficient, and superficially hard, Gilly manages to do just what she wants until she is sent to stay with Maime Trotter, a woman with a big heart, patience, and wisdom enough to know how to reach the unhappy girl.

1978 Award

Bridge to Terabithia   Katherine Paterson
Illustrated by Donna Diamond   Crowell

After practicing all summer to be the fastest runner in school, Jess is beaten by the new girl, Leslie. Gradually the two become close friends, creating an imaginary world in the woods and calling it Terabithia. When tragedy strikes, Jess, shocked and despairing, slowly begins to see the wonders Leslie left him.

HONORS

Ramona and Her Father. Beverly Cleary. Illustrated by Alan Tiegreen. Morrow.

Ramona is in second grade when her father loses his job and her mother begins to work full-time. Ramona tries her best to help her family through the crisis, even starting a campaign to get her father to quit smoking. Her worries, problems, and joys, presented with lively good humor, are common to many children her age.

Anpao: An American Indian Odyssey. Jamake Highwater. Illustrated by Fritz Scholder. Lippincott.

A beautiful Indian maiden promises to marry Anpao, but first he must get the Sun's permission and have him remove the ugly scar on his face. As Anpao travels the world looking for the Sun, he hears stories about his own roots as well as legends and myths of his people.

1977 Award

Roll of Thunder, Hear My Cry
Mildred D. Taylor   Dial

Cassie Logan and her brothers are part of a warm, intelligent, and coura-geous black family in rural Mississippi during the Depression. They try to maintain their pride as they take abuse from white children and then recog-nize that their personal difficulties are only symptoms of greater problems within their community.

HONORS

A String in the Harp. Nancy Bond. Atheneum.

Their father's remoteness and the strangeness of school in Wales make the children's adjustment to their mother's death even more difficult. Then twelve-year-old Peter finds an ancient harp key that pulls him back into Welsh history, helping him discover a purpose to living.

Abel's Island. William Steig. Farrar.

After a violent storm, Abel, a mouse, finds himself alone, bewildered, and far, far away from his beloved wife Amanda. Sustained by his love for his wife, Abel uses all his resources to survive for a year on the deserted island.

1976 Award

The Grey King   Susan Cooper
Illustrated by Michael Heslop   McElderry / Atheneum

In Wales recovering from a serious illness, eleven-year-old Will, the youn-gest of the Old Ones, uses his considerable powers to find the golden harp that will awaken the Sleepers. It is not an easy quest, and Will has only the mysterious Bran and Bran's dog, Cafall, to help him fight the forces of dark and evil.

HONORS

The Hundred Penny Box. Sharon Bell Mathis. Illustrated by Leo and Diane Dillon. Viking.

For each of her hundred years there is a penny in Aunt Dew's box and a story to go along with it. More than his parents, Michael understands the impor-tance of the box to the old woman and loves to hear her tell the stories again and again.

Dragonwings. Laurence Yep. Harper.

In 1903 Moonshadow leaves the Middle Kingdom to join his father in San Francisco. To make the father's dream of building an aeroplane come true, the two of them leave the close-knit community that shelters their Chinese culture to live among white demons. Humorous accommodations are made between the different cultures as they grow in understanding and friendship.

1975 Award

M. C. Higgins, the Great
Virginia Hamilton   Macmillan

Up on Sarah's Mountain, M. C. dreams of a way for his family to escape the spoil heap that may one day destroy their home. It is not his dreams but the boy's own strength and determination that help the family find a way to keep themselves safe.

HONORS

My Brother Sam Is Dead.   James Lincoln Collier and Christopher Collier. Four Winds.

Tim's older brother, Sam, defies their father and runs off to join the Continental Army. When their father is imprisoned by the rebels and dies and Sam is hung by his own army, Tim sees how devastating war can be.

Philip Hall Likes Me, I Reckon Maybe.   Bette Greene.   Illustrated by Charles Lilly.   Dial.

Eleven-year-old Beth Lambert, a spunky heroine, realizes she has been letting Philip Hall be number one in school because she is afraid he will not like her if she surpasses him. With gentle prodding from her family, Beth decides to go ahead and do her best—even if it means beating Philip Hall.

The Perilous Gard.   Elizabeth Marie Pope.   Illustrated by Richard Cuffari. Houghton.

Banished by Queen Mary to the remote castle of Elvenwood, Kate Sutton quickly learns the castle's secret: It guards the last practitioners of the old religions. To keep their power, the fairy folk decide to sacrifice the man Kate loves on All Hallow's Eve.

Figgs & Phantoms.   Ellen Raskin.   Dutton.

Mona is embarrassed by her zany, ex-show business family—except for her four-foot-four-inch-tall Uncle Florence Italy Figg. When he dies, Mona is desolate. She is sure he has gone to Capri, the Figg family Heaven, and decides to follow him.

1974 Award

The Slave Dancer   Paula Fox
Illustrated by Eros Keith   Bradbury

Kidnapped and forced to play his fife while the slaves "dance," thirteen-year-old Jessie learns all too soon about the savagery of the slave trade.

For four long months he lives with the crew's cruelty until a storm wrecks the ship and Jessie and Ras, a would-be slave, are the only survivors.

HONOR

The Dark Is Rising. Susan Cooper. Illustrated by Alan Cober. McElderry/Atheneum.

On midwinter's eve, Will's eleventh birthday, the world is in turmoil with strange creatures appearing and stranger things happening. Will, the last of the Old Ones to be born, must use all his knowledge and skill to help in the fight against the Dark.

1973 Award

Julie of the Wolves   Jean Craighead George
Illustrated by John Schoenherr   Harper

Having run away from a forced marriage, thirteen-year-old Miyax, an Eskimo, becomes lost on the Arctic plain. Her only hope for survival is acceptance by a wolf pack. Imitating their facial expressions and body movements, Miyax slowly becomes one of them, while still trying to get to safety.

HONORS

Frog and Toad Together. Arnold Lobel. Harper.

Whether they are testing their willpower with a bowl of cookies or their patience while waiting for seeds to grow, Frog and Toad delight in each other's company. Witty, easy-to-read, and full of warmth and gentle humor, these five stories engagingly explore the meaning of friendship.

The Upstairs Room. Johanna Reiss. Crowell.

As the German occupation of Holland tightens, two Jewish sisters are forced to hide in a secret upstairs room in an old farmhouse for two years. The girls experience fear, hope, terror, and boredom in their daily life and depend on the kindness and courage of others for their survival.

The Witches of Worm. Zilpha Keatley Snyder. Illustrated by Alton Raible. Atheneum.

Deserted by her friends and her mother, Jessica channels her anger at life into "evil acts" that her cat, Worm, supposedly forces her to perform. Convinced first that Worm is a witch's cat, then that she is a witch, Jessica is ultimately forced to face herself and her feelings.

1972 Award

Mrs. Frisby and the Rats of NIMH   Robert C. O'Brien
Illustrated by Zena Bernstein   Atheneum

When nothing she does seems to help her son Timothy get well, Mrs. Frisby, a widowed mouse, turns to a colony of super-intelligent rats for help. The rats' high intelligence is the result of experiments performed upon them by human scientists at NIMH. Now the rats are intent upon starting a new civilization free from human interference.

HONORS

Incident at Hawk's Hill.   Allan W. Eckert.   Illustrated by John Schoenherr. Little, Brown.

Lonely, small, and frail, six-year-old Ben shies away from people but shows deep interest in and affinity toward animals. Lost during a storm, he takes refuge with a badger who has just lost her young. The badger adopts him, and he lives a feral life for three months until he is found. Convincingly written, the incident is based on an actual occurrence in 1870.

The Planet of Junior Brown.   Virginia Hamilton.   Macmillan.

For more than two months, huge, musical genius Junior Brown and his friend and protector Buddy Clark have been cutting classes and hiding in a secret basement room created by the school custodian. Buddy and Mr. Poole, the custodian, are trying desperately to help Junior, who seems to be slipping slowly but inexorably into madness.

The Tombs of Atuan.   Ursula K. LeGuin.   Illustrated by Gail Garraty. Atheneum.

From the time Tenar was five, her life has been focused on the tombs and her future as their priestess. Renamed Arha, she guards the labyrinthine tunnels, knowing that they hide great treasure. When she finds a man (Ged of *A Wizard of Earthsea*) in the tunnels seeking the other half to the Ring of Erreth-Akbe, Arha is torn between her duty to kill him and her compassion for him.

Annie and the Old One.   Miska Miles.   Illustrated by Peter Parnall. Little, Brown.

Annie likes her life the way it is with her mother weaving, her father making jewelry, and her grandmother, the Old One, always there to tell her stories and to help with chores. When grandmother announces that she will die when the new rug is finished, Annie tries desperately to stop the inevitable by secretly unraveling the rug.

The Headless Cupid.   Zilpha Keatley Snyder.   Illustrated by Alton Raible. Atheneum.

Eleven-year-old David is pleased about his father's remarriage until he meets his new stepsister, Amanda, a self-proclaimed witch. Angry at her mother for remarrying, Amanda sets up situations that lead the other children to believe their house is haunted. Then unexplained events turn the tables, frightening even Amanda.

1971 Award

Summer of the Swans Betsy Byars
Illustrated by Ted CoConis Viking

An insecure fourteen-year-old, Sarah is unhappy with herself and her family. Though she loves her mentally disabled brother Charlie, Sarah is tired of always being responsible for him. When Charlie turns up missing, however, Sarah tries desperately to find him and in the process discovers that she is less the ugly duckling than she had supposed.

HONORS

Knee Knock Rise. Natalie Babbitt. Farrar.

In this tale filled with folk humor, Egan goes to the village for a visit and becomes intrigued with the tales and wails of a monster that lives in the peaks of Knee Knock Rise. After an unprecedented climb up the mountain, Egan discovers the practical explanation for the legendary creature. The villagers refuse to listen to him, preferring to let their folklore live on as history.

Enchantress from the Stars. Sylvia Louise Engdahl. Illustrated by Rodney Shackell. Atheneum.

Invaded by technologically advanced Imperials, the Andrecians are close to being destroyed by their occupiers when beings from an even more highly advanced civilization decide to intervene secretly. Using their telekenetic powers, three Federation members pose as magicians, teaching a young Andrecian how to use his psychic abilities to combat the invaders.

Sing Down the Moon. Scott O'Dell. Houghton.

At fourteen, Bright Morning dares to be optimistic about her future. Her mother is a wealthy Navajo, and Bright Morning is to marry Tall Boy, a young Navajo warrior. Then she is wrenched from her home by Spanish slavers. When freed, she is uprooted again, this time by the cavalry, who force the Navajo to make a 300-mile march to Bosque Redondo.

1970 Award

Sounder William H. Armstrong
Illustrated by James Barkley Harper

Sounder, the family dog, valiantly defends the father when the sheriff and his deputies come to arrest him for stealing food for his starving family. Years later, the dog, shot and maimed by the deputies, is the only one to recognize the father when he returns, paralyzed and deformed.

HONORS

Our Eddie. Sulamith Ish-Kishor. Pantheon.

Eddie's father is a stern, insensitive zealot who refuses, until it is too late, to see that his son is gradually succumbing to a debilitating disease. Set in London and New York in the 1920s, most of this story of a warm Jewish immigrant family is told by Eddie's insightful sister.

The Many Ways of Seeing: An Introduction to the Pleasures of Art.
Janet Gaylord Moore.   Illustrated with black-and-white and
color reproductions and photographs.   World.

Moore, of the Cleveland Museum of Art, encourages readers to try a new way of approaching art: to see art reflecting the world and nature, and the world in turn reflecting art. Paintings (reproduced in color), poems, and quotations are arranged to lead to the discovery of new comparisons between modern, traditional, or ancient art and the imagery of word and picture.

Journey Outside.   Mary Q. Steele.   Illustrated by Rocco Negri.   Viking.

In a story filled with allegory and symbolism, Dilar's people endlessly travel an underground river, headed for the "better place." But Dilar, suspecting that they are merely going around in circles, jumps from his raft and accidentally makes his way into the outside world. There, nearly blinded by the light, he tries to learn more about his people and to find a way to bring them aboveground.

1969 Award

The High King
Lloyd Alexander   Holt

In the final book of the chronicles of Prydain, Taran leads his forces against Arawn and his army of the dead. Victorious, but with great loss of life and destruction to Prydain, Taran becomes High King, fulfilling the predictions of his wizard guardian, Dallben.

HONORS

To Be a Slave.   Julius Lester.   Illustrated by Tom Feelings.   Dial.

American slaves, runaways, and emancipated people provide a powerful testament of how they felt about slavery and what they endured. The author dynamically blends quotations from published and unpublished sources and presents them in rough chronological order.

When Shlemiel Went to Warsaw and Other Stories.   Isaac Bashevis Singer.
Illustrated by Margot Zemach.   Farrar.

In eight delightfully silly stories, five retold from the Yiddish and three original, readers are introduced to a memorable collection of characters. Among them are a mixed-up Shlemiel, who does not recognize his wife and village, and Utzel's daughter, Poverty, who seems to grow larger as he grows poorer.

1968 Award

From the Mixed-Up Files of Mrs. Basil E. Frankweiler
E. L. Konigsburg   Atheneum

Having carefully planned how and to where they will run away, Claudia and her little brother, James (and his money), board a bus, head to New York City, and go to the Metropolitan Museum of Art. There they hide in washrooms, sleep on ancient beds, and get involved in solving an exciting mystery.

HONORS

Jennifer, Hecate, Macbeth, William McKinley, and Me, Elizabeth.
   E. L. Konigsburg.   Atheneum.

Elizabeth is lonely at her new school until she meets Jennifer, a girl her age who claims to be a real witch. In awe of Jennifer, Elizabeth agrees to become her apprentice and initially finds her boring life full of adventure. But Jennifer is very demanding, and even superficially docile Elizabeth can only be pushed so far.

The Black Pearl.   Scott O'Dell.   Illustrated by Milton Johnson.   Houghton.

In this story written with stark simplicity and riveting suspense, Ramon confronts his two greatest enemies in the waters of Baja California. The legendary curse of the Manta Diablo holds true when Ramon wrests the fabulous black pearl from the Manta's cave and his life is changed forever.

The Fearsome Inn.   Isaac Bashevis Singer.   Illustrated by Nonny Hogrogian.   Scribner.

Unaware that the owners of the inn are a witch and her half-devil husband, three young men seek shelter there on a stormy winter night. One of the three, a clever student of the Cabala, recognizes the couple's evil and courageously defeats them, sending the pair "behind the Mountains of Darkness where there is neither day nor night."

The Egypt Game.   Zilpha Keatley Snyder.   Illustrated by Alton Raible.   Atheneum.

April and Melanie begin the Egypt game in the backyard of a slightly sinister curio shop. With costumes, ceremonies, an evil god, an oracular owl, and four other members, the game is seriously and imaginatively played. After the murder of a child, they are forced inside for awhile, but finally they begin the game again. This time one of the players almost becomes the next victim.

1967 Award

Up a Road Slowly
Irene Hunt   Follett

When Julie is seven, her mother dies. She and her little brother are sent to live with her strict, schoolteacher aunt. Through the years, Julie keeps hoping that her father will want them back, that staying with Aunt Cordelia is just temporary, but slowly she comes to love her aunt and wants to stay.

HONORS

The King's Fifth.   Scott O'Dell.   Illustrated by Samuel Bryant.   Houghton.

Imprisoned in Vera Cruz and awaiting trial, seventeen-year-old Esteban tells of his part in the disastrous expedition for gold to the Seven Cities of Cibola. A mapmaker, Esteban is left with the bags of gold. After seeing the greed, cruelty, and, finally, death of those searching for it, he throws the gold into a volcanic crater.

Zlateh the Goat and Other Stories.   Isaac Bashevis Singer.   Illustrated by Maurice Sendak.   Harper.

Seven stories rich with eastern European culture and Jewish folklore are filled with lively characters, delightfully funny fools, clever people, and loyal animals. The ink drawings of Sendak create wonderful scenes complementing the stories perfectly.

The Jazz Man.   Mary Hays Weik.   Illustrated by Ann Grifalconi. Atheneum.

Night after night Zeke and his mother and father listen to the jazz man play his piano. Then his mother tires of his father not working, and she leaves them. Soon his father goes as well, and Zeke is alone. As the gloomy days and nights pass, Zeke dreams of the jazz man and of better, happier times.

1966 Award

I, Juan de Pareja
Elizabeth Borton de Trevino   Farrar

Behind the great painter Velasquez stands his faithful slave, Juan, ready to prepare a canvas, mix paint, and boost his morale. But, secretly, Juan teaches himself to paint, winning his freedom and the respect of a great master.

HONORS

The Black Cauldron.   Lloyd Alexander.   Holt.

Assistant Pig-Keeper Taran excitedly joins Gwydion and the other men of Prydain in their attack on Arawn, Lord of Annuvin, and his cauldron-born army. Only by destroying the cauldron can they hope to stop Arawn and his deathless warriors from overrunning Prydain.

The Animal Family. Randall Jarrell. Illustrated by Maurice Sendak.
Pantheon.
Isolated in his house by the sea, the hunter is lonely until the day he sees the
mermaid. Together they form an amazing family with first a bear cub, then a
lynx, and finally an orphaned boy. Each fits gently and beautifully into the
very special world created by the unusual couple.

The Noonday Friends. Mary Stolz. Illustrated by Louis Glanzman. Harper.
Her hard-working mother and out-of-work father depend on Franny to take
care of her little brother after school and to help out in other ways. The only
time left for friendship is during lunch hour at school when she talks to
Simone, a friend with whom she can share problems.

—————————————— **1965 Award** ——————————————

Shadow of a Bull   Maia Wojciechowska
Illustrated by Alvin Smith   Atheneum

With everyone waiting for him to become a great bullfighter like his father,
Manolo is afraid to let them know that he has a different dream—to become
a doctor. He trains and practices for the ring until finally he has the courage
and confidence to admit that he can never be a bullfighter.

HONOR

Across Five Aprils. Irene Hunt. Follett.
At nine, Jethro is excited by the prospect of a civil war coming to the country.
When the nation really does go to war, his brothers and friends go in different
directions, fighting for either the North or the South. Jethro begins to understand how devastating war really is to family and nation.

—————————————— **1964 Award** ——————————————

It's Like This, Cat   Emily Neville
Illustrated by Emil Weiss   Harper

When his father suggests that owning a dog might be good for him, fourteen-year-old Dave defiantly goes to Aunt Kate the Cat Woman and adopts
a stray. The cat ends up leading him to new people and adventures all over
Manhattan—and even to an appreciation for his parents.

HONORS

Rascal: A Memoir of a Better Era. Sterling North. Illustrated by
John Schoenherr. Dutton.
For twelve months Sterling owned the raccoon, raising him from a tiny captured kit to a large adult yearning for his freedom. Bright, curious, energetic,
and endearing, Rascal fills the boy's life with love, companionship, and adventure during their year together.

The Loner. Ester Wier. Illustrated by Christine Price. McKay.

Both nameless and homeless, the boy wanders the country with other migrants, hoping to find work and food. Finally, lost and weak from hunger, he collapses and is found by a woman called The Boss. The gruff but gentle sheep rancher names him David and gives him a chance to make his own life on her Montana ranch.

--------------------------------- **1963 Award** ---------------------------------

A Wrinkle in Time
Madeleine L'Engle   Farrar

Meg, Charles Wallace, and next-door neighbor Calvin go into space and through time to rescue Meg's father, a scientist who disappeared while working on a secret project. The children's intergalactic search leads them to a confrontation with the forces of evil on the planet Camazotz, where conformity means survival.

HONORS

Thistle and Thyme: Tales and Legends from Scotland. Sorche Nic Leodhas, pseud. (Leclaire Alger). Illustrated by Evaline Ness. Holt.

Using her memories of stories told in her family, the author retells ten stories based on Scottish legends and folktales. Some are humorous, others mysterious and suspenseful, and all of them possess the rhythm of the Gaelic language.

Men of Athens. Olivia Coolidge. Illustrated by Milton Johnson. Houghton.

The golden age of Greece comes to life through the men and women who lived during and immediately before and after that brief fifty-year period. The battles they waged to make Greece strong and free; the brilliance of the leading artists, philosophers, and statesmen; and the excitement of the time make exciting reading.

--------------------------------- **1962 Award** ---------------------------------

The Bronze Bow
Elizabeth George Speare   Houghton

At the death of his parents, Daniel swears vengeance against the Roman invaders. For five years he hides in the mountains of Galilee with a band of rebels but finally must return to care for his sister. He meets Jesus but refuses to accept his message of love, wanting revenge instead. Only when all seems nearly lost does he start to understand the power of love.

HONORS

Frontier Living. Edwin Tunis. World.

Beginning with the settlement of the Piedmont area in the early 1700s, nineteen distinct frontier movements take American settlers from the East Coast across the continent and through the nineteenth century. Details of daily life and carefully drawn pictures of the people and objects show what makes this era unique.

The Golden Goblet. Eloise Jarvis McGraw. Coward.

Under the control of his cruel and unscrupulous half-brother, Gebu, Ranofer, a boy of ancient Egypt who lives in Thebes, is sent to work for a goldsmith. Slowly he discovers that Gebu is stealing gold objects from the Valley of the Tombs, and he must find a way to expose him.

Belling the Tiger. Mary Stolz. Illustrated by Beni Montresor. Harper.

Asa and Rambo, the two smallest mice, are given the dubious honor of belling the cat. While getting the bell, the two accidentally get stuck on a ship and travel to a tropical island where they "bell" a tiger. Home again, the diminutive duo have the courage to demand a raise in status.

1961 Award

Island of the Blue Dolphins
Scott O'Dell   Houghton

Accidentally left behind when her tribe flees, Karana spends eighteen years alone on an island off the coast of California. Her courage and resourcefulness help her to survive and to fill her life with moments of beauty and happiness.

HONORS

America Moves Forward: A History for Peter. Gerald W. Johnson.
Illustrated by Leonard Everett Fisher. Morrow.

From World War I to 1956, major events and important men of politics are evaluated and discussed for their impact on American life and history. The third and final volume in a work that offers a personalized look at American history, the book is illustrated with striking scratchboard pictures.

Old Ramon. Jack Schaefer. Illustrated by Harold West. Houghton.

Old Ramon teaches the boy as much as he can during the months they spend with the sheep in the mountains. Along the way, Ramon shares stories of his youth as a shepherd with the boy's grandfather and brings the boy back to the valley with a keener understanding and appreciation for the life of a shepherd.

The Cricket in Times Square. George Selden, pseud. (George Thompson). Illustrated by Garth Williams. Farrar.

Accidentally brought into a New York City subway station, Chester Cricket is found by Mario Bellini, the son of a newsstand owner. Chester is befriended by two subway animals, Harry Cat and Tucker Mouse, who encourage him to use his musical talents to help the Bellinis. An overnight success, Chester nonetheless longs to return to the country.

1960 Award

Onion John   Joseph Krumgold
Illustrated by Symeon Shimin   Crowell

Twelve-year-old Andy is torn between his love for his father and his affection for Onion John, the old man whose way of life is totally foreign to nearly everyone in town. When members of the Rotary Club try to build Onion John a new house, their actions have great repercussions.

HONORS

My Side of the Mountain. Jean Craighead George. Dutton.

Tired of living in a crowded city apartment, Sam Gribley runs away from home and heads for his Grandpa Gribley's long-lost homestead in the Catskill mountains. For a year he stays alone, learning to live off the land, hollowing out a tree for a home, taming a falcon, and using every bit of ingenuity and resourcefulness he has to survive.

America Is Born: A History for Peter. Gerald W. Johnson. Illustrated by Leonard Everett Fisher. Morrow.

Johnson's account of America's history is a very personal retelling of the lives and adventures of the people who explored and settled this country. The first in a three-volume series, the book covers the time from Columbus to the Revolutionary War and the Constitutional Convention.

The Gammage Cup. Carol Kendall. Illustrated by Erik Blegvad. Harcourt.

Five misfits are sent into exile in the mountains when they refuse to conform to Minnepin traditions of dress, ideas, and life-style. They come to the rescue of the Land Between the Mountains when they uncover an invasion plot by the Mushroom People.

1959 Award

The Witch of Blackbird Pond
Elizabeth George Speare   Houghton

When her grandfather dies, sixteen-year-old Kit leaves the West Indies to live with her Puritan Aunt Rachel and her family. Kit's lively personality, her bright clothes, and her friendship with an outcast Quaker woman make her a target for charges of witchcraft in 1687 New England.

HONORS

The Family under the Bridge.   Natalie S. Carlson.   Illustrated by
Garth Williams.   Harper.

Armand, who wanders the streets of Paris without a care, finds that his place beneath a bridge has been invaded by three children and their mother. Though he does not want to have anything to do with the children, the old man soon becomes a grandfather figure to the family, helping them, sharing the fun of the city, and ultimately making them his responsibility.

Along Came a Dog.   Meindert DeJong.   Illustrated by Maurice Sendak.
Harper.

When her frostbitten toes fall off, the little red hen becomes a target for the other chickens' abuse. Only the big, homeless dog comes to her rescue, looking on her as something to guard and love as he tries to make the farm his home.

Chucaro: Wild Pony of the Pampa.   Francis Kalnay.   Illustrated by
Julian de Miskey.   Harcourt.

Once wild on the Argentine pampa, Chucaro is captured and tamed by Pedrito and his gaucho friend Juan. When the patron demands a gentle horse for his spoiled and cruel son, it is Chucaro he gets in spite of Pedrito's determination to keep him.

The Perilous Road.   William O. Steele.   Illustrated by Paul Galdone.   Harcourt.

Eleven-year-old Chris passionately hates the Yankees invading his Tennessee homeland and wants to do anything to help the South. He is deaf to his father's words when he says war is the worst thing that can happen to people. Then Chris is caught in the middle of a savage battle and realizes how horrible war really is.

─────────────── **1958 Award** ───────────────

Rifles for Watie
Harold Keith   Crowell

Sixteen-year-old Jeff, already a combat veteran in the Union Army and winner of the Congressional Medal of Honor, is captured by the rebel troops of General Stand Watie, a Cherokee Indian, and forced to become one of his scouts.

HONORS

Gone-Away Lake.   Elizabeth Enright.   Illustrated by Beth and Joe Krush.
Harcourt.

All summer Julian and his ten-year-old cousin Portia explore the houses they discover around Gone-Away Lake. They tell no one about the place or the two old people living in one of the houses until a near tragedy exposes their secret.

Tom Paine, Freedom's Apostle. Leo Gurko. Illustrated by Fritz Kredel. Crowell.

With hardly any education or money and only Ben Franklin's letter of introduction, Tom Paine goes to America and writes *Common Sense*, the first of his revolutionary pamphlets. The power and vision of Paine's writings and the violent feelings they aroused throughout his life are evident in this biography.

The Great Wheel. Robert Lawson. Viking.

Aunt Honoria predicts that Conn will leave Ireland and head west. Now he is in Chicago working on a construction project for a man named Ferris. His aunt has also made the wild prediction that he will ride the world's biggest wheel. Conn does as soon as Mr. Ferris's daring project is completed for the Chicago World's Columbian Exposition of 1893.

The Horsecatcher. Mari Sandoz. Westminster.

Unlike the other Cheyenne boys, Young Elk refuses to kill. He wants to capture and tame the wild horses of the prairie. When his father insists he join in their war, he runs away, returning months later with fifteen horses and the start of what becomes a nearly legendary way with wild horses.

1957 Award

Miracles on Maple Hill   Virginia Sorensen
Illustrated by Beth and Joe Krush   Harcourt

When her father finally returns from being a prisoner of war, Marley's family decides to try to make a new beginning on a beautiful farm in Pennsylvania. During their first year there, they marvel at the miracle of the sap rising in the maple trees and the changes in each other.

HONORS

Black Fox of Lorne. Marguerite de Angeli. Doubleday.

Shipwrecked off the coast of medieval Scotland, identical twins Jan and Brus are the only ones left alive when their father and his men are murdered. They survive by tricking the Scots into thinking that only one of them exists. Having sworn to avenge their father's murder, they foil the man's treasonous plot and keep their vow.

The House of Sixty Fathers. Meindert DeJong. Illustrated by Maurice Sendak. Harper.

Alone in his family sampan, Tien Pao lands in Japanese-occupied China and begins a dangerous journey back to Hengyang during World War II. On his way, a company of American airmen adopt him, and he finds himself with sixty strange but kind fathers who help him find his family.

Old Yeller. Fred Gipson. Illustrated by Carl Burger. Harper.

Left to help care for the homestead while his father takes their cattle to Kansas, fourteen-year-old Travis initially resents the intrusion of the big yellow dog. The dog proves his worth by rescuing little Arliss from a bear and Travis from wild hogs, guaranteeing himself a home.

Mr. Justice Holmes. Clara Ingram Judson. Illustrated by Robert Todd. Follett.

The son of a famous writer, Oliver Wendell Holmes, Jr. is a daydreamer whose brilliance is not always apparent to his family. After serving in the Civil War, he becomes a lawyer and a teacher, trying to make law interesting and clear to those entering the profession. Well-respected but never wealthy, he becomes one of the country's most highly esteemed Supreme Court justices.

The Corn Grows Ripe. Dorothy Rhoads. Illustrated by Jean Charlot. Viking.

A happy but often irresponsible twelve-year-old Yucatan boy must suddenly grow up when his father is injured. Tigre bravely goes to another village to get a bonesetter and then sets about clearing and burning the family's new corn field, a ritualized duty that goes back to Mayan times. He proves he can be reliable.

1956 Award

Carry On, Mr. Bowditch Jean Lee Latham
Illustrated by John O'Hara Cosgrove Houghton

In spite of having little education, Nat Bowditch manages to teach himself mathematics and the principles of navigation. When he gets the chance to sail as a second mate, he teaches the rest of the crew to navigate and even finds mistakes in the navigational tables. He later rewrites the tables, and they become a standard navigational tool.

HONORS

The Golden Name Day. Jennie Lindquist. Illustrated by Garth Williams. Harper.

Staying with her Swedish-American grandparents while her mother is hospitalized, Nancy is warmly welcomed into an extended family of aunts, uncles, and cousins. With everyone else having a special Swedish Name Day to celebrate, the family unsuccessfully tries to find a matching Swedish name for Nancy. Only when a new family moves in is Nancy's problem solved.

The Secret River. Marjorie Kinnan Rawlings. Illustrated by Leonard Weisgard. Scribner.

When hard times come to the Florida forest people, little Calpurnia and her dog, Buggyhorse, go to the wise woman of the forest for help. Advised to follow her nose, Calpurnia discovers a beautiful river full of fish. She catches many and brings them home, making hard times "soft."

Men, Microscopes, and Living Things. Katherine Shippen. Illustrated by Anthony Ravielli. Viking.

The author begins with Aristotle and his investigation of natural science, then moves on to Pliny, Harvey, Linnaeus, Lamarck, and others. The lively yet factual writing provides interesting insights into the work of significant biologists.

1955 Award

The Wheel on the School   Meindert DeJong
Illustrated by Maurice Sendak   Harper

Inspired by Lina's composition about storks, her classmates and teacher decide to find a way to bring the birds and their luck back to their little Dutch village. As the children involve the people of the village in the search for a wheel and for a way to attach it to their school, they bring their small community together.

HONORS

Courage of Sarah Noble. Alice Dalgliesh. Illustrated by Leonard Weisgard. Scribner.

"Keep up your courage," Sarah's mother tells her when she leaves with her father to build a home in the wilderness. The home finished, Sarah stays with friendly Indians while her father goes back for the rest of the family.

Banner in the Sky. James Ullman. Lippincott.

Although his father died trying to climb the Citadel, the highest mountain in the Alps, Rudy is determined to scale it himself. He hides his climbing ability from his mother and his Alpine-guide uncle and joins an English expedition hoping to be able to plant his father's red shirt at the top as a banner in the sky.

1954 Award

. . . And Now Miguel   Joseph Krumgold
Illustrated by Jean Charlot   Crowell

Every spring Miguel hopes this is the year he will be asked to join the men as they take their sheep up into the Sangre de Cristo Mountains of New Mexico. When at the age of twelve he is told it is not yet time for him, he works hard and prays that his father will see how grown up he is.

HONORS

All Alone. Claire Huchet Bishop. Illustrated by Feodor Rojankovsky. Viking.

When his father sends him to the high pastures with the heifers, Marcel is forcefully reminded of the village motto, "Each man for himself." But loneliness makes the yodel of another boy welcome, and when disaster strikes, Marcel is saved by his willingness to help someone else.

Magic Maize. Mary and Conrad Buff. Illustrated by the authors. Houghton.
With the gringo world encroaching on the old ways of the Indians of Guatemala, a father continues to teach his son the old ways of farming and of praying to the gods of planting and harvest. Yet when their crop fails, it is the gringos who come to the family's aid.

Hurry Home, Candy. Meindert DeJong. Illustrated by Maurice Sendak. Harper.
Taken from his mother before he is weaned and given to a family that only knows how to hurt and control him, Candy is lost on a family outing and becomes a stray. He longs for his own home and for people who will really love him.

Shadrach. Meindert DeJong. Illustrated by Maurice Sendak. Harper.
After Davie's grandfather promises him a rabbit of his own, the little boy's excitement is nearly uncontainable. Davie bravely gathers food near a dangerous Dutch canal, helps get his hutch ready, and, when the rabbit arrives, lavishes attention and affection on the little animal.

Theodore Roosevelt, Fighting Patriot. Clara Ingram Judson. Illustrated by Lorence F. Bjorklund. Follett.
Independent and honorable, Theodore is forever facing challenges because of his poor health, bad vision, and determination to learn as much as he can. As an adult he is remembered for leading the Rough Riders up San Juan Hill, starting our national park system, and being a president with tremendous courage and integrity.

1953 Award

Secret of the Andes   Ann Nolan Clark
Illustrated by Jean Charlot   Viking

Determined to discover another way of life, Cusi leaves his beautiful Incan home in the Andes Mountains and goes to the lowlands of Spanish Peru. Once there he longs for the hidden valley and the Old One. He returns knowing that he will never again willingly leave his home or break his vow to keep the Incan secret.

HONORS

The Bears on Hemlock Mountain. Alice Dalgliesh. Illustrated by Helen Sewell. Scribner.
"There are no bears on Hemlock Mountain, no bears at all," Jonathan repeats as he goes over the mountain to borrow the big iron pot. But on the way back, Jonathan learns that there are indeed bears on Hemlock Mountain.

Birthdays of Freedom, Vol. I.   Genevieve Foster.   Scribner.

Starting with the excitement of the signing of the Declaration of Independence, the author sweeps back in time to the cave dwellers. From that time to the fall of Rome in 476 A.D., the determination to gain freedom is shown as the spark that encourages great inventions, discoveries, and political movements.

Moccasin Trail.   Eloise Jarvis McGraw.   Illustrated by Paul Galdone.   Coward.

A runaway who is clawed by a grizzly and left for dead, Jim is raised by the Crow Indians and becomes a mountain man. Receiving a letter from his little brother asking for help, Jim finds his orphaned family on a wagon train heading to Oregon. He agrees to stay with them on the dangerous journey west. It is Jim's courage and Crow training that help them survive.

Red Sails to Capri.   Ann Weil.   Illustrated by C. B. Falls.   Viking.

Three wealthy strangers come to Michele's small island village and stay at his parents' inn. Their good spirits and desire for adventure soon convince Michele and his friends to help the strangers explore a forbidden cave. Their discovery of the now-famous Blue Grotto changes the lives of everyone on Capri.

Charlotte's Web.   E. B. White.   Illustrated by Garth Williams.   Harper.

After being raised by the farmer's daughter, Wilbur, a pig, is sold to another farm where his companion is a gray spider named Charlotte. When it becomes apparent that Wilbur is being fattened up for slaughtering, Charlotte promises to save him. The words that begin appearing in Charlotte's web amaze the farmer and bring hope to Wilbur.

--- **1952 Award** ---

Ginger Pye
Eleanor Estes   Harcourt

The only clue to the mysterious disappearance of Ginger, the Pye family dog, is the unusual man in the mustard-colored hat. Jerry and Rachel look everywhere for their little dog, occasionally seeing the mustard-hatted man, and finally solve the mystery of Ginger's disappearance.

HONORS

Americans before Columbus.   Elizabeth Baity.   Illustrated by C. B. Falls. Viking.

A study of pre-Columbian peoples in the Americas, this book describes their art, architecture, music, literature, and culture from the earliest times to that of Columbus. The text is prefaced with photographs of art and architecture and includes ink drawings in every chapter.

The Apple and the Arrow.   Mary and Conrad Buff.   Houghton.

Caught by tyrant Gessler's soldier, Walter's father, William Tell, is forced to either shoot an apple on Walter's head or die. He successfully shoots the apple but is imprisoned. Breaking free, Tell kills Gessler and starts the revolution that wins Switzerland's freedom.

Minn of the Mississippi. Holling C. Holling. Houghton.
Over a twenty-five-year period a snapping turtle makes her way from the source of the Mississippi to the Delta. Along the way she encounters a variety of adventures, lays eggs as she grows older, and introduces readers to the varied people, places, and wildlife along the river.

The Defender. Nicholas Kalashnikoff. Illustrated by Claire and George Louden. Scribner.
In turn-of-the-century Siberia, Turgen, a widowed hunter and herbalist, becomes the target of the local shaman when he begins to protect the shy, fast-disappearing mountain rams. Turgen's only friends are a poor widow, whom he befriends and marries, and her two children.

The Light at Tern Rock. Julia L. Sauer. Illustrated by Georges Schreiber. Viking.
Although Mr. Flagg has promised to get them back to shore by December 15, Aunt Martha and Ronnie suddenly realize that they are stuck at the lonely lighthouse until after Christmas. At first angry and sullen, Ronnie finally joins Aunt Martha in a very special celebration of the holiday.

──────────────── **1951 Award** ────────────────

Amos Fortune, Free Man   Elizabeth Yates
Illustrated by Nora S. Unwin   Dutton
Captured by slavers, Amos, son of an African king, survives the long ocean voyage only to be sold to a New England Quaker. After years of serving and learning from others, Amos buys his own freedom, sets up his own business, and begins to buy and set free other slaves.

HONORS

Gandhi, Fighter without a Sword. Jeanette Eaton. Illustrated by Ralph Ray. Morrow.
From an upper-class life in India, Gandhi travels to England where he becomes a lawyer. Later he goes to South Africa and becomes involved in fighting for civil liberties. Back in India, Gandhi spends the remainder of his life leading the nonviolent independence movement, which finally brings freedom to India and martyrdom to Gandhi.

Better Known as Johnny Appleseed. Mabel Leigh Hunt. Illustrated by James Daugherty. Lippincott.
Loved by the settlers and the Indians, John Chapman carves a new name and legend for himself by trekking through the wilderness planting apple trees

and helping anyone in need. The few facts known about Chapman are carefully interwoven with the Johnny Appleseed legends.

Abraham Lincoln, Friend of the People. Clara Ingram Judson. Illustrated with drawings by Robert Frankenberg and Kodachromes of the Chicago Historical Society Lincoln Dioramas. Follett.

Vividly written and carefully researched, the book portrays the struggles Abraham Lincoln has in learning to read, making a living, and finally entering politics. The difficulties of life on the frontier and the problems leading to the Civil War form the background.

The Story of Appleby Capple. Anne Parrish. Harper.

For his Cousin Clement's ninety-ninth birthday, five-year-old Appleby is determined to give the old man the thing he wants most to see: a zebra butterfly. The boy wanders through the alphabet looking for the butterfly. Ink illustrations work people and objects around all twenty-six letters.

1950 Award

The Door in the Wall
Marguerite de Angeli   Doubleday

Crippled by a strange disease, Robin is ready to give up since he knows he will never be a knight. Then the monks help him to find ways to gain strength and courage and ultimately to play an important role in saving his medieval city.

HONORS

Tree of Freedom. Rebecca Caudill. Illustrated by Dorothy B. Morse. Viking.

During the American Revolution, the Venable family leaves North Carolina to seek new land and get away from British oppression. Their exciting month-long trek over the mountains to Kentucky starts them on the way to new freedom, symbolized by the apple tree, whose seeds have come with the family all the way from France.

The Blue Cat of Castle Town. Catherine Coblentz. Illustrated by Janice Holland. Longmans.

Born under a blue moon, the little kitten is destined to carry the river's song of beauty, peace, and contentment to the unhappy people of Castle Town, Vermont. They have exchanged beauty for money, no longer making things with honesty and unable to "sing their own songs."

George Washington. Genevieve Foster. Scribner.

Filled with interesting excerpts from letters and diaries, this animated portrayal of the first president of the United States tells of George Washington's childhood and his many challenges as surveyor, soldier, commander in chief, and president.

Song of the Pines: A Story of Norwegian Lumbering in Wisconsin. Walter and Marion Havighurst. Illustrated by Richard Floethe. Winston.

An orphan, fifteen-year-old Nils joins the Svendsen family and other Norwegian emigrants as they head toward America in the 1850s. They travel to Wisconsin where they stake out a claim for a farm. Nils, having found work in the lumber camps, creates his own business and future in America.

Kildee House. Rutherford Montgomery. Illustrated by Barbara Cooney. Doubleday.

Not used to talking or being around people, Jerome Kildee retires to a small house he builds atop a hill in the redwood forest of northern California. Through the animals he shelters and the young people he meets, Kildee's life and the lives of those he encounters become fuller and richer than he ever imagined.

1949 Award

King of the Wind Marguerite Henry
Illustrated by Wesley Dennis   Rand McNally

Sure that the motherless Arabian colt is going to be a great racer, Agba, the Sultan's mute slaveboy, raises the animal and stays with it, even when the horse is sent to France. Times are hard for the two, and they are often treated cruelly, but Agba never gives up his belief in the horse that becomes the ancestor of the great Man o' War.

HONORS

Story of the Negro. Arna Bontemps. Illustrated by Raymond Lufkin. Knopf.

Beginning with the first slave ship to come to Jamestown, Bontemps celebrates the culture and accomplishments of black people throughout the world: from the cultural heritage of Africa to the artists, leaders, and momentous events that have shaped not only black but world culture as well.

My Father's Dragon. Ruth S. Gannett. Illustrated by Ruth Chrisman Gannett. Random House.

An old alley cat convinces the narrator's father to rescue a baby dragon being used as a ferry by the animals of far-away Wild Island. With chewing gum, toothpaste, lollipops, and ribbons, the little boy keeps lions and tigers from eating him as he tries to rescue the little dragon.

Seabird. Holling C. Holling. Houghton.

To help him while away the hours on the whaling ship, Ezra carves a mascot, Seabird, which becomes his constant companion as he journeys around the world and finally gets his own ship. For four generations Seabird brings companionship and luck to Ezra's family as they sail the sea.

Daughter of the Mountain.   Louise Rankin.   Illustrated by Kurt Wiese.   Viking.

When Momo's beloved Lhasa terrier is stolen by a wool trader, the Tibetan girl follows him on a long and dangerous journey that takes her through the mountains into India and finally to Calcutta.

1948 Award

The Twenty-One Balloons
William Pène du Bois   Viking

Professor Sherman leaves San Francisco in one hot air balloon and three weeks later is found in the Atlantic Ocean, clinging to the remains of twenty balloons and refusing to tell how he got there.

HONORS

The Quaint and Curious Quest of Johnny Longfoot.   Catherine Besterman. Illustrated by Warren Chappell.   Bobbs-Merrill.

Sent to the country to stay with his very thrifty uncle, Johnny, son of the shoe king, outwits guard dogs and a bear to reach the miserly old man. Not welcome, he goes on a quest that leads him to a cat who sends him to look for gold and seven-league boots. Leading a band of dogs, cats, bears, and his tagalong uncle, Johnny resourcefully succeeds in his mission.

Pancakes-Paris.   Claire Huchet Bishop.   Illustrated by Georges Schreiber. Viking.

Before the war there was heat and food and paper. Now Charles wishes for a way to show his little sister the fun of Mardi Gras and the wonderful crepes they ate. When two American soldiers suddenly enter his life and give him a strange box that they claim holds the ingredients for crepes, things start to happen.

The Cow-tail Switch, and Other West African Stories.   Harold Courlander. Illustrated by Madye Lee Chastain.   Holt.

Puns, trickster tales, creation tales, parables, and proverbs form the basis for these seventeen stories from West Africa. Faithfully retold from original sources, the stories are great fun to read or tell.

Li Lun, Lad of Courage.   Carolyn Treffinger.   Illustrated by Kurt Wiese. Abingdon.

When Li Lun refuses to join his father on his trip out to sea, the man angrily sends the boy up to the top of their mountain to grow rice. Alone on the mountaintop for 120 days, Li Lun, called a coward by his father and the other boys, courageously faces the elements, determined to complete his task.

Misty of Chincoteague.   Marguerite Henry.   Illustrated by Wesley Dennis. Rand McNally.

When Pony Penning Day comes on Chincoteague Island, Maureen and Paul are determined to buy the Phantom and her filly, Misty. They work hard and save $102, and finally the two spirited animals are theirs. Now the children must train the wild ponies to be around people, instead of running wild on Assateague.

―――――――――――― **1947 Award** ――――――――――――

Miss Hickory   Carolyn Sherwin Bailey
Illustrated by Ruth Gannett   Viking

With an apple twig for a body and a hickory nut for a head, Miss Hickory stubbornly refuses help as she tries to survive a cold New Hampshire winter alone.

HONORS

Wonderful Year. Nancy Barnes. Illustrated by Kate Seredy. Messner.

Eleven-year-old Ellen and her fun-loving parents move from an easy life in Kansas to a ranch in western Colorado. They enjoy life as they plant trees and build a home and a barn. For Ellen, the best part is her friendship with fifteen-year-old Ronnie and the adventures they share.

Big Tree. Mary and Conrad Buff. Viking.

A glorious tree that can live thousands of years and has no fear of fire or insects, the redwood Wawona begins to grow long before the pyramids and the coming of Christ. Nothing threatens the huge and ancient tree until man arrives with axes and saws. But others recognize his importance and offer protection to the redwood.

The Avion My Uncle Flew. Cyrus Fisher, pseud. (Darwin L. Teilhet). Illustrated by Richard Floethe. Appleton.

When John's father returns home after World War II, he decides to take his wife and son to France. There John will have a chance to get his injured leg treated and to see his mother's homeland. John does not want to go, but he has no choice. Once there he becomes involved in a mysterious adventure that takes him to southern France and his glider-building uncle.

The Heavenly Tenants. William Maxwell. Illustrated by Ilonka Karasz. Harper.

The night before the Maxwells are to leave for three weeks in Virginia, father takes the children outside and shows them the different constellations that make up the zodiac. When no one comes to care for their animals while they are gone, the signs of the zodiac come to Earth and do it for them.

The Hidden Treasure of Glaston. Eleanore Jewett. Illustrated by Frederick T. Chapman. Viking.

When he is forced to leave the country because of his part in the murder of Thomas à Becket, Sir Hugh de Morville leaves his crippled son in the care of the monks at Glaston. As the boy and a new friend explore the area, they discover treasure left by King Arthur and his court and begin an exciting and suspenseful search for the Holy Grail.

---------------------------- **1946 Award** ----------------------------

Strawberry Girl
Lois Lenski   Lippincott

Birdie's family wants to make a good living growing strawberries and oranges in turn-of-the-century Florida. Unfortunately their shiftless neighbors, the Slaters, fight them every step of the way.

HONORS

Justin Morgan Had a Horse.   Marguerite Henry.   Illustrated by Wesley Dennis. Rand McNally.

Justin Morgan does not want the little colt that follows him and Joel home. But Joel raises and trains it, and the two soon realize that the little horse is something very special, not to mention very fast. Years later it becomes the first of a new breed: the Justin Morgan horse.

The Moved-Outers.   Florence Crannell Means.   Illustrated by Helen Blair. Houghton.

After the attack on Pearl Harbor, the Ohara family, who have always thought of themselves as Americans, are suddenly "Japanese." Put into internment camps with only the barest of necessities, Sue and her family try not only to survive but to stay loyal Americans.

New Found World.   Katherine Shippen.   Illustrated by C. B. Falls.   Viking.

A history of Latin America, the book begins with a chapter on the topography and the plant and animal life of the area. Additional chapters discuss the native peoples and their interaction with European explorers and colonists. Well-researched, the book covers aspects of Latin American life and history up to the end of World War II.

Bhimsa, the Dancing Bear.   Christine Weston.   Illustrated by Roger Duvoisin. Scribner.

While aimlessly walking in his Indian garden, David is surprised by the approach of a boy, Gopala, and his tame bear, Bhimsa. He eagerly runs away with the two as they wander through India trying to find a way home for Gopala. Bhimsa's dancing attracts attention everywhere, earning them food and getting them into and out of trouble along the way.

1945 Award

Rabbit Hill
Robert Lawson   Viking

The excitement among the wild creatures is contagious as Little Georgie enthusiastically tells every one of them that new folks are coming to the old farmhouse. All of the animals anxiously await the day the newcomers will arrive, afraid they might be the kind who have guns or dogs or even poison.

HONORS

The Silver Pencil.   Alice Dalgliesh.   Illustrated by Katherine Milhous. Scribner.

After her father's sudden death, Janet and her mother begin a series of moves that take them from Trinidad, to England, to the United States, and then to Nova Scotia. Along the way, Janet holds fast to the silver pencil her father gave her, finding that writing is a solace.

Lone Journey: The Life of Roger Williams.   Jeanette Eaton.   Illustrated by Woodi Ishmael.   Harcourt.

From childhood onward, Roger Williams is a champion for religious freedom. Again and again he speaks out for separation of church and state, risking his own life and trying to save the lives of others. Finally Williams becomes the founder of the Providence Colony in America, where settlers of all religious faiths can find refuge.

The Hundred Dresses.   Eleanor Estes.   Illustrated by Louis Slobodkin. Harcourt.

Wanda Petronski, who speaks in broken English and always wears the same sparkling clean dress to school each day, brags to the other girls that she has a hundred dresses at home. Wanda is laughed at and teased by the other girls, and she and her family move away. Only then do the girls find Wanda's beautifully drawn pictures of one hundred dresses.

Abraham Lincoln's World.   Genevieve Foster.   Scribner.

As Abraham Lincoln grows from birth to death, the things happening throughout the world affect him and his country. Chapter by chapter the stories of not only Lincoln but also Napolean, Jefferson, Tecumseh, Jackson, Bismarck, and others are told alternately to give a full and fascinating picture of world events.

1944 Award

Johnny Tremain   Esther Forbes
Illustrated by Lynd Ward   Houghton

Fourteen-year-old apprentice silversmith Johnny Tremain has a terrible accident that forces him to give up his work. He becomes involved with Sam

Adams and the other Boston patriots, takes part in the Boston Tea Party, and plays a role in the battle of Lexington.

HONORS

Rufus M. Eleanor Estes. Illustrated by Louis Slobodkin. Harcourt.

A lively and imaginative little boy, Rufus is the youngest of the four Moffat children. Anxious to do his part for the war effort, he knits washcloths, plants a victory garden, and earns enough money selling popcorn to become a Victory Boy.

Fog Magic. Julia Sauer. Illustrated by Lynd Ward. Viking.

In every generation of Addingtons there is one person for whom the dense fog of Nova Scotia is magical. Walking toward the deserted village of Blue Cove on a foggy day, Greta comes upon a thriving village she has never seen before. It is the Blue Cove of one hundred years ago.

These Happy Golden Years. Laura Ingalls Wilder. Illustrated by Helen Sewell and Mildred Boyle. Harper.

Laura Ingalls, though still a student herself, begins teaching in small schools and sewing to earn tuition money for Mary's education. Whether working hard in town, teaching, living on her family's claim on the Dakota prairie, or finally deciding to marry Almanzo, Laura realizes how lucky she is to have her warm, happy family.

Mountain Born. Elizabeth Yates. Illustrated by Nora S. Unwin. Coward.

Nursed back to life by Peter's mother, Biddy, a black lamb, is given to six-year-old Peter to raise. Bright and brave, Biddy becomes the leader of the herd, repeatedly alerting her human keepers to impending disaster.

———————————— 1943 Award ————————————

Adam of the Road Elizabeth Janet Gray
Illustrated by Robert Lawson Viking

Adam, his minstrel father, their horse, and Adam's trained dog, Nick, are traveling in thirteenth-century England, singing and telling stories for food and a place to sleep. When Nick is stolen, father and son try desperately to find him and become separated from each other.

HONORS

The Middle Moffat. Eleanor Estes. Illustrated by Louis Slobodkin. Harcourt.

Janey is the "middle Moffat," trying hard to be serious and to do everything well. Things do not seem to work out quite as she plans (her organ recital turns into an escape for thousands of moths), but the little girl is undeterred. She continues to make bold plans with outrageously funny results.

"Have You Seen Tom Thumb?" Mabel Leigh Hunt. Illustrated by
Fritz Eichenberg. Lippincott.

From the age of five, Charles Sherwood Stratton, only twenty-five inches tall
and weighing fifteen pounds, is presented to the world by P. T. Barnum as
General Tom Thumb. A charming, humorous person, he travels all over the
world with Barnum.

1942 Award

The Matchlock Gun Walter Edmonds
Illustrated by Paul Lantz Dodd

Edward, his mother, and his little sister have only one defense against the
French and the Indians—a huge matchlock gun. When attacked, his mother
is wounded, and Edward must use the gun to save their lives.

HONORS

George Washington's World. Genevieve Foster. Scribner.

From birth to death, the story of George Washington's life and the lives of
other well-known kings, soldiers, politicians, and scientists of the same
period are interwoven. In each section the author skillfully provides a
worldview of events.

Down Ryton Water. Eva Roe Gaggin. Illustrated by Elmer Hader. Viking.

Escaping the religious persecution of their English countrymen, Matt and his
family and neighbors head down Ryton Water for freedom in Holland.
Finally ready to face the long and dangerous voyage to the New World, all of
them board the *Mayflower* and *Speedwell* to sail to what becomes the Plymouth Colony.

Indian Captive: The Story of Mary Jemison. Lois Lenski. Lippincott.

Even though other settlers have been slaughtered by the French and the Indians, Pa refuses to let his family go east to safety. They, too, are captured, and
only young, blond-haired Mary survives, forced to become a part of the Sen-
eca people.

Little Town on the Prairie. Laura Ingalls Wilder. Illustrated by Helen
Sewell and Mildred Boyle. Harper.

Laura is fifteen and, in warm weather, working hard with Ma and Pa on their
Dakota Territory claim. She earns what she can to help pay for Mary's courses
at the College for the Blind, and, with her family, she spends the long, cold,
but friend-filled winters in town.

---------------------------- **1941 Award** ----------------------------

Call It Courage
Armstrong Sperry   Macmillan

Mocked by the other boys because of his fear of the sea, Mafatu secretly takes a small boat and leaves his village. Alone on a terrifying ocean voyage, the boy, son of a Polynesian chief, overcomes his fear of the sea.

HONORS

Young Mac of Fort Vancouver.   Mary Jane Carr.   Illustrated by Richard Holberg.   Crowell.

Traveling west to Fort Vancouver in 1832, Young Mac is determined to become a fur-trading Northman and not a full-fledged member of the white world. Contact with Dr. McLoughlan, head of the fort, and other white and mixed-heritage men causes him to reconsider his decision.

Blue Willow.   Doris Gates.   Illustrated by Paul Lantz.   Viking.

With her small family wandering from place to place so that Dad can find work, Janey has never really had a home or school or friends. Maybe the San Joaquin Valley will be the place where everything changes, a place where they can stay and she can finally bring the blue willow plate out for good.

Nansen.   Anna Gertrude Hall.   Illustrated by Boris Artzybasheff.   Viking.

Determined to learn as much as he can as a little boy (and even more determined as an adult), Fridtjof Nansen grows to be one of Norway's most famous citizens. He is an explorer who travels all the way to the North Pole, a statesman, and, most difficult of all, a fighter for world peace and a winner of the Nobel Peace Prize.

The Long Winter.   Laura Ingalls Wilder.   Illustrated by Helen Sewell and Mildred Boyle.   Harper.

The Ingalls family, pioneering in the Dakota Territory, stoically endure a dreary succession of blizzards. Huddled in the family store, they and their neighbors must depend upon their ingenuity to prevent freezing and starvation.

---------------------------- **1940 Award** ----------------------------

Daniel Boone
James Daugherty   Viking

A rugged frontiersman and a leader of pioneers, Daniel Boone starts life in Pennsylvania and ends it eighty-six years later in Missouri, an almost legendary character. Boone's longing for adventure, his bravery, and his foolishness are examined honestly in this biography that sings the praises of pioneer men and women in words and vigorous drawings.

HONORS

Boy with a Pack. Stephen W. Meader. Illustrated by Edward Shenton. Harcourt.

Bill fills a backpack with things to sell in Ohio and, with two years of savings, leaves his New Hampshire mill town on foot. The 1837 journey is long and hard but filled with all kinds of adventures, danger, and amazing good luck.

Runner of the Mountain Tops: The Life of Louis Agassiz. Mabel Robinson. Illustrated by Lynd Ward. Random House.

A brilliant naturalist and the founder of Harvard's Agassiz Museum, Louis Agassiz is realistically portrayed from his childhood in Switzerland through his years as a Harvard professor. Agassiz's fascination with all of nature and his great teaching ability are evident throughout the book.

The Singing Tree. Kate Seredy. Viking.

Four years after the end of *The Good Master,* the First World War has started, and Mother, Jancsi, and cousin Kate are left to take care of the farm as Father and Uncle Sandor are called to fight. The three of them hold the farm together and make it a refuge for orphans, relatives, and even prisoners of war.

By the Shores of Silver Lake. Laura Ingalls Wilder. Illustrated by Helen Sewell and Mildred Boyle. Harper.

The Ingalls have not had a good crop since the grasshoppers came. Pa decides they will make one more move, this time to Dakota Territory. The family spends a happy winter taking in other settlers and earning money to send Mary, blind from scarlet fever, to a special school.

1939 Award

Thimble Summer
Elizabeth Enright   Farrar & Rinehart

All kinds of good things seem to happen after Garnet finds the silver thimble in the dried-up river bed. The nine-year-old farm girl notices that the drought finally breaks, she has an exciting time being locked in the public library with a friend, and her pet pig wins a blue ribbon at the fair.

HONORS

Nino. Valenti Angelo. Viking.

While his father works in America to earn their fare to California, Nino and his mother stay with his grandfather in his small Italian village. The little boy and his family and friends share holidays, trips to the city, and small but exciting adventures that create a memorable picture of turn-of-the-century Italy.

Mr. Popper's Penguins. Richard and Florence Atwater. Illustrated by Robert Lawson. Little, Brown.

From the moment he is given a penguin as a pet, Mr. Popper's life starts changing. He converts his basement into an ice rink, finds a friend for his lonely bird, and suddenly has twelve penguins to feed instead of one.

"Hello the Boat!" Phyllis Crawford. Illustrated by Edward Laning. Holt.

The entire Doak family pitches in to get their store-boat from Pittsburgh to Cincinnati in 1817. Along the Ohio River, settlers shout out, "Hello the boat!" and the family eagerly pushes the boat ashore and enthusiastically opens the store. On their way, the Doaks encounter thieves, learn about the history of the river area, and have a surprisingly good time.

Leader by Destiny: George Washington, Man and Patriot. Jeanette Eaton. Illustrated by Jack Manley Rose. Harcourt.

Not a man who plans what he wants but rather one who allows things to shape him and his future, George Washington lives a life full of adventure and responsibility as he grows up. The fifty-two years of his life that Eaton covers contain much of the history and many of the famous people of his time.

Penn. Elizabeth Janet Gray. Illustrated by George Gillett Whitney. Viking.

Until he converts to the Quaker religion, William Penn leads a privileged upper-class life. Then he loses everything and is imprisoned. After fighting hard for religious freedom, Penn is allowed to go to America and found the new colony of Pennsylvania, based on the principles for which he fought.

--------------------- **1938 Award** ---------------------

The White Stag   Kate Seredy   Viking

Based on legends about the founding of Hungary, this stirring story begins with Nimrod receiving a prophesy from God. He tells his people to follow the White Stag and Nimrod's sons to the west. During their long and dangerous journey, the people move valiantly westward until the birth of Attila, who one day leads them heroically into what becomes Hungary.

HONORS

Pecos Bill. James Cloyd Bowman. Illustrated by Laura Bannon. Little, Brown.

Raised by coyotes and able to speak to animals, Pecos Bill reluctantly accepts the knowledge that he is one of those dreaded inhuman humans. He becomes a cowboy and does things in legendary proportion: busting up a cyclone, breaking up a cattle rustling gang, and rounding up 39,000,000 cattle and driving them to market.

Bright Island. Mabel Robinson. Illustrated by Lynd Ward. Random House.

Strong, independent, and committed to life on her family's small island off the coast of Maine, Thankful very reluctantly agrees to attend school on the mainland. There, life is so foreign that she initially feels like a total outsider among the other high school students.

On the Banks of Plum Creek. Laura Ingalls Wilder. Illustrated by Helen Sewell and Mildred Boyle. Harper.

After finally reaching Minnesota and planting a wheat crop, the Ingalls lose it to a horde of grasshoppers. Determined to stay, Pa goes to work for other farmers. Laura goes to school, shares adventures with friends, but most of all enjoys the moments when her family is together and Pa is back playing the fiddle.

1937 Award

Roller Skates   Ruth Sawyer
Illustrated by Valenti Angelo   Viking

Her wealthy parents in Europe, Lucinda spends a glorious year living with two teachers, skating all over New York City, and making friends everywhere. The people she meets, whether it is her impoverished musician neighbor or the hansom cab driver, appreciate her energy, friendliness, and determination.

HONORS

The Golden Basket. Ludwig Bemelmans. Viking.

A staid English father and his two little daughters visit Bruges, Belgium, and stay at the Golden Basket Hotel. The girls and the hotel owner's son enjoy exploring the famous city. While visiting a cathedral, they meet twelve little girls standing in two straight lines, the youngest and spunkiest being Madeline.

Winterbound. Margery Bianco. Viking.

With both of their parents gone for months, nineteen-year-old Kay and sixteen-year-old Garry take on managing both the rented cottage and their younger brother and sister. During a long, cold, but very exciting depression-era winter, they make friends, earn and save money, and gain strength and independence.

The Codfish Musket. Agnes Hewes. Illustrated by Armstrong Sperry. Doubleday.

Even as a youngster, Dan has a keen eye for fine rifles and arms. On a mission to Washington for his Boston employer, Dan becomes secretary to Thomas Jefferson. The president sends him into the frontier with a message for Merriwether Lewis, but along the way Dan spots gun thieves arming the Indians. He defeats them and delivers his message, finally returning to Washington.

Whistler's Van. Idwal Jones. Illustrated by Zhenya Gay. Viking.

After his grandfather disappears one night with a cart and pony, Gwilyn decides he wants a chance to wander through Wales as well. When the Ringos, a family of gypsies, appear at the farmhouse and whistle, Gwilyn goes off with them for a summer full of music, adventure, and, most importantly, horses.

Phebe Fairchild: Her Book. Lois Lenski. Stokes.

When Phebe's mother decides to join Phebe's father on a sea voyage, the ten-year-old is sent to stay with relatives in the country. Life in 1830 rural Connecticut at first seems rigid to Phebe, and her copy of Mother Goose is a constant source of support. The child comes to appreciate her relatives, their simple life, their generosity, and their sense of fun.

Audubon. Constance Rourke. Illustrated by James MacDonald. Harcourt.

Despite mysterious beginnings, John James Audubon manages to leave France and go to America. He marries but continues to traipse the countryside in search of birds and small animals to paint. Carefully researched, the book offers a well-rounded look at the man who became known for his nineteenth-century paintings of American birds.

1936 Award

Caddie Woodlawn   Carol Ryrie Brink   Macmillan

Eleven years old in 1864, Caddie roams the woods and rivers of western Wisconsin with her brothers as her mother relentlessly tries to make her into a young "lady." The mischievous redhead's adventures with Indians and pioneers are full of fun and excitement.

HONORS

Young Walter Scott. Elizabeth Janet Gray. Viking.

Despite years of living with country relatives, Walter is determined not to let his lame leg stand in his way once he is at home again. This lively, fictionalized biography transports readers to late eighteenth-century Edinburgh, Scotland, and offers an engrossing introduction to the life of the famous novelist.

The Good Master. Kate Seredy. Viking.

Jancsi is fascinated by his city cousin Kate's daring and reckless behavior. Whether she is stopping a stampede of horses, nearly drowning in the river, or running off with gypsies, she is a marvel and a delight to the Hungarian country folk.

All Sail Set: A Romance of the Flying Cloud. Armstrong Sperry. Winston.

Fifteen-year-old Thach goes to work for the great Donald McKay making drawings of his plans for the clipper ship *Flying Cloud*. The ship completed, Thach becomes an apprentice, sails around the Horn, is initiated by "Neptune," contends with mutineers, and nearly loses his life in a shipboard fire.

Honk, the Moose. Phil Stong. Illustrated by Kurt Wiese. Dodd.

The temperature is thirty below zero and the snow is seven feet deep when the boys find a moose in Ivar's father's stable. The town is in an uproar as everyone tries to think of ways to get the gentle and very funny beast to leave.

──────────────── **1935 Award** ────────────────

Dobry   Monica Shannon
Illustrated by Atanas Katchamakoff   Viking

Bulgarian peasant boy Dobry tries to convince his mother that he must be an artist. He does not want to plow the fields as his ancestors did. Dobry's grandfather understands, but until Dobry sculpts a beautiful nativity scene in the snow to prove his talents, his mother is not convinced.

HONORS

Davy Crockett. Constance Rourke. Illustrated by James MacDonald. Harcourt.

Davy Crockett is a bigger-than-life character: he is a pioneer, hunter, teller of tales, soldier, statesman, and legendary American hero. Rourke writes a well-researched and well-documented biography filled with anecdotes and comments by Crockett and his contemporaries.

Pageant of Chinese History. Elizabeth Seeger. Illustrated by Bernard Watkins. Longmans.

Using a conversational style, Seeger leads the reader through Chinese history starting with mythical and legendary times. Then she writes about each of the dynasties, ending with the Manchu in 1912 and the beginning of the republic. Political and cultural history are the focus of most of the book.

A Day on Skates: The Story of a Dutch Picnic. Hilda Van Stockum. Harper.

The canals of Holland are finally frozen solid, and the headmaster has a surprise. He takes the children on an all-day skating picnic. In spite of a few accidents, it is a thoroughly enjoyable time. Many black-and-white drawings and eight full-color illustrations show the festive atmosphere of the day.

──────────────── **1934 Award** ────────────────

Invincible Louisa: The Story of the Author of Little Women
Cornelia Meigs   Little, Brown

The life of Louisa May Alcott is chronicled through her lively involvement with family and friends. Incidents reveal that her invincible spirit keeps the family afloat during the darkest of times and always keeps them happy. Family photographs and a chronology are included.

HONORS

The Winged Girl of Knossos.   Erick Berry, pseud. (Allena Best).   Appleton.

Spirited, athletic, and beautiful Inas, daughter of Daidalos, helps her father with his flying experiments on the Isle of Crete during the time of King Minos. Having to leave Crete hurriedly, she does so by flying out on a glider built by her father.

The Big Tree of Bunlahy: Stories of My Own Countryside.   Padraic Colum. Illustrated by Jack Yeats.   Macmillan.

Twelve fine old Irish tales and one original one are woven together by the storyteller who introduces each story. All are said to have been heard under the Tree of Bunlahy, the great elm tree with big, smooth stones under it. There the villagers would sit and listen to these tales of animals, heroes, and leprechans.

The ABC Bunny.   Wanda Gág.   Coward.

Lithographs filled with curved lines show a bunny romping through his day. After being scared out of his bed by a crashing apple, the bunny meets many animals. Each large, bright red letter of the alphabet is accompanied by a text that carries the ABC lesson along in a rhythmic manner. The song, with words and music, is included.

Glory of the Seas.   Agnes Hewes.   Illustrated by N. C. Wyeth.   Knopf.

The exciting early days of the clipper ships, the controversial Fugitive Slave Law, and the inner conflict caused by civil disobedience are at the center of this story set in Boston in the 1850s. When the *Flying Cloud* sails to San Francisco in just eighty-nine days, many Bostonians dream of sailing to California.

The Apprentice of Florence.   Anne Kyle.   Illustrated by Erick Berry, pseud. (Allena Best).   Houghton.

Nemo, a sixteen-year-old Florentine apprentice, is sent to Constantinople on business in 1453. The city is besieged by Turks, and Nemo is hurt. On his return, young Christopher Columbus tells him that his father, thought to be dead, is alive. More adventures ensue as Nemo searches for his lost father.

New Land.   Sarah Schmidt.   Illustrated by Frank Dobias.   McBride.

It is the 1930s when Dad, the seventeen-year-old twins, and their younger sister arrive in Wyoming to homestead on an unproved claim. Rivalries on the football field and in the new vocational school, a blinding snowstorm, and troubles with the "big man" are overcome, and a new home is established.

Swords of Steel.   Elsie Singmaster.   Illustrated by David Hendrickson. Houghton.

Although he has heard talk of the differences between the North and the South, it is not until 1859, when his beloved, free black friend is kidnapped to be sold, that John feels personal involvement in the conflict. In six years John grows from childhood to manhood with the Civil War intruding on and then enveloping his life.

The Forgotten Daughter. Caroline Snedeker. Illustrated by
Dorothy P. Lathrop. Doubleday.

When his wife dies in childbirth while he is traveling, the Roman centurion is told that both mother and child are dead. His daughter is subjected to the hardships of second-century life as a slave. Eventually she falls in love with a high-born Roman, and the plague unites her with her father.

1933 Award

Young Fu of the Upper Yangtze — Elizabeth Lewis
Illustrated by Kurt Wiese — Winston

The empress has died and political life is in turmoil when Young Fu and his mother move from their village to Chungking so that he can be apprenticed to a coppersmith. Young Fu must constantly use his wits to protect his mother and himself from thieves and rascals.

HONORS

Children of the Soil: A Story of Scandinavia. Nora Burglon. Illustrated by
Edgar Parin d'Aulaire. Doubleday.

Two very poor but ambitious and industrious children live with their mother in Sweden at the turn of the twentieth century. The soil they hoe is poor, their crab trap washes out to sea, and a weaving contest is lost to the gentry. With a little help from a Tomte and a lot of work on their part, they acquire some livestock and the promise of a happier future.

Swift Rivers. Cornelia Meigs. Illustrated by Forrest W. Orr. Little, Brown.

When his mean-spirited uncle locks him out of the house where he was raised, Chris knows it is time to become a man. The harsh 1835 Wisconsin winter and the bountiful woods lead him to try floating logs down to St. Louis. As a part of the early days of the logging industry, Chris has many adventures on the river.

The Railroad to Freedom: A Story of the Civil War. Hildegarde Swift.
Illustrated by James Daugherty. Harcourt.

Harriet Tubman, a slave, escapes from the South but goes back again and again, leading three hundred other slaves North to freedom via the dangerous Underground Railroad. The horrifying yet often thrilling adventures are based on incidents from Tubman's life.

1932 Award

Waterless Mountain — Laura Adams Armer
Illustrated by Sidney and Laura Armer — Longmans

Destined to become a medicine man, introspective Younger Brother learns the songs and stories of the Navajo Indians and begins to create songs of his own. Skillfully interwoven into the story are the early twentieth-century culture and heritage of the tribe.

HONORS

Jane's Island. Marjorie Allee. Illustrated by Maitland de Gorgoza. Houghton.

Ellen, a college freshman, spends the summer with twelve-year-old Jane in Woods Hole, Massachusetts, where Jane's father is a marine biologist. The girls enjoy light summer adventures while fishing and picnicking. Jane is a competent naturalist who imparts a good measure of scientific information throughout the story.

Truce of the Wolf and Other Tales of Old Italy. Mary Gould Davis. Illustrated by Jay Van Everen. Harcourt.

Seven widely varied Italian stories tell of such things as Saint Francis taming a menacing wolf, of an obstinate and heroic donkey, and of how a street in Florence was named. The tales, all told with a bit of Italian folk humor, come from many sources, including a Tuscan peasant woman and *The Decameron*.

Calico Bush. Rachel Field. Illustrated by Allen Lewis. Macmillan.

In 1743, twelve-year-old Marguerite is bound out to a family in Maine. Discriminated against by the parents because she is French, she finds happiness with the children as they all face hardships and the rigors of life in the Maine wilderness.

The Fairy Circus. Dorothy P. Lathrop. Macmillan.

When the circus tent goes up, it is so big that it encloses the places where the fairies live. They all scramble for the best view, and when it is over they decide to have a circus of their own. The fairies and woodland animals use grand imaginations as they re-create the circus in their own way.

Out of the Flame. Eloise Lownsbery. Illustrated by Elizabeth Tyler Wolcott. Longmans.

In the sixteenth century, Pierre is first a page then a squire as he becomes trained to be a knight in the court of Francis I. He attends tournaments, visits with great intellectuals, and learns music and botany with the royal children. Before the story ends, he and the children are abducted and released by pirates.

Boy of the South Seas. Eunice Tietjens. Illustrated by Myrtle Sheldon. Coward-McCann.

When a ship arrives in the harbor of the Marquesas Islands, young Teiki's curiosity gets ahold of him, and he climbs aboard and falls asleep. He awakens when the vessel is under sail and there is no turning back. At the island of Moorea, he swims ashore and makes a new life for himself.

1931 Award

The Cat Who Went to Heaven Elizabeth Coatsworth
Illustrated by Lynd Ward Macmillan

A starving Japanese artist is commissioned to paint the death of Buddha. He longs to include his gentle cat, Good Fortune, among the animals, but legend says cats cannot enter heaven. Because of her goodness, he paints her, and the little animal dies of happiness. When the priest objects, the painting miraculously changes to show Buddha accepting the cat.

HONORS

Mountains Are Free. Julia Davis Adams. Illustrated by Theodore Nadejen. Dutton.

Bruno, a young Swiss orphan who is being raised by the Tells, suddenly decides to become a page to an Austrian, saying he will return when he can earn his own way. The stirring of democracy causes conflicts as the Swiss try to rebel against the harshness of their Habsburg rulers.

Garram the Hunter: A Boy of the Hill Tribes. Herbert Best. Illustrated by Erick Berry, pseud. (Allena Best). Doubleday.

Hoping to find an ally for his chieftain father, Garram is sent to stay with the emir and becomes a favorite of the ruler. When he returns home, he discovers not only a plot to imprison his father but receives word that the eastern tribes are threatening.

Meggy MacIntosh. Elizabeth Janet Gray. Illustrated by Marguerite de Angeli. Doubleday.

In 1775 orphaned fifteen-year-old Meggy leaves her native Scotland to sail for the colony of North Carolina. There she joins Flora MacDonald, who had helped Bonnie Prince Charlie escape. Meggy becomes involved in the revolutionary cause and moves away from Flora, a loyalist.

Spice and the Devil's Cave. Agnes Hewes. Illustrated by Lynd Ward. Knopf.

At a workshop in Portugal, Bartholomew Diaz, Vasco da Gama, and Ferdinand Magellan gather to discuss their theory that an all-sea route around the Cape of Good Hope, also known as the Devil's Cave, must exist. The theft by pirates of the only known maps adds interest and intrigue.

Queer Person. Ralph Hubbard. Illustrated by Harold von Schmidt. Doubleday.

He can neither hear nor talk, and at age four he wanders into a camp of Pikuni Indians. His silence earns him the name Queer Person, and he is raised by an old woman in the tribe. During his test of bravery, he rescues the chief's lost son from the Crows, and it is revealed that they are brothers.

Ood-Le-Uk the Wanderer. Alice Lide and Margaret Johansen. Illustrated by Raymond Lufkin. Little, Brown.

An Alaskan Eskimo caught on an ice floe crosses the Bering Straight. After years of wandering, he returns home to establish trade between his tribe and the Siberian tribesmen. Once known as a weakling, after his hazardous adventures he is known to be a brave man.

The Dark Star of Itza: The Story of a Pagan Princess. Alida Malkus. Illustrated by Lowell Houser. Harcourt.

When the khan of Chichén Itzá kidnaps the betrothed of another Mayan chieftain, war breaks out, and the city falls into the hands of the Toltecs. The seventeen-year-old daughter of Chichén Itzá's chief priest agrees to be the sacrifice that will save her city, but her father bravely finds a way to save her.

Floating Island. Anne Parrish. Harper.

All packed up and on board a ship bound for the tropics, a doll family and their doll house land on Floating Island after their ship wrecks. They adapt well to the island but soon realize that dolls can never be happy if they are away from children for too long. They then arrange their own rescue.

─────────────── **1930 Award** ───────────────

Hitty, Her First Hundred Years   Rachel Field
Illustrated by Dorothy P. Lathrop   Macmillan

Carved from a block of mountain ash a hundred years before, the six-and-a-half-inch doll now sits secure in the antique shop window and writes her memoirs. She recounts the adventures she had with many different people in places around the world. Illustrations show Hitty in many styles of clothing in her life thus far.

HONORS

Vaino. Julia Davis Adams. Illustrated by Lempi Ostman. Dutton.

Ancient legends of Finland, the lives of three children, and the Finnish Revolution of 1917 are blended together to tell a story filled with strong patriotic spirit. Vaino and his older brother and sister become a part of the revolution that finally frees Finland of foreign domination.

A Daughter of the Seine: The Life of Madame Roland. Jeanette Eaton. Harper.

Madame Roland's life coincides with the French Revolution. The historical biography describes the childhood, married life, and tragic execution by guillotine of this remarkable woman. Madame Roland is intelligent and strongly supports the revolution, and her salon is depicted as the headquarters of much political activity.

The Jumping-Off Place.   Marian Hurd McNeely.   Illustrated by William Siegel.   Longmans.

When the uncle who cared for them dies, four children pull up stakes in Wisconsin and move to South Dakota. There they weather adventures, hardships, and squatters for the fourteen months it takes to make homesteaders owners of the land.

Pran of Albania.   Elizabeth Miller.   Illustrated by Maud and Miska Petersham. Doubleday.

In post-World War I Albania amidst a threat of attack from Slavs, fourteen-year-old Pran falls in love. Rather than submit to an arranged marriage, she vows to never marry. After a truce is made, Pran realizes the man she loves is the same man her parents had arranged for her to marry.

Little Blacknose.   Hildegarde Swift.   Illustrated by Lynd Ward.   Harcourt.

Little Blacknose is none other than the DeWitt Clinton Engine, the first locomotive built for the New York Central Railway. The personified engine tells of his life until he becomes enthroned in New York's Grand Central Terminal.

The Tangle-Coated Horse and Other Tales.   Ella Young.   Illustrated by Vera Bock.   Longmans.

The Fionn Saga, the stories of Finn McCool known in every Gaelic-speaking part of Scotland and all over Ireland, is retold with vigor. The stories begin when McCool is a small boy learning about his heritage and his crafts and end three hundred years later when his son returns from the country of the Ever-Young.

1929 Award

The Trumpeter of Krakow   Eric P. Kelly
Illustrated by Angela Pruszynska   Macmillan

For two hundred years the Charnetski family has guarded Poland's most famous jewel. When the czar of Russia finds out about the valuable crystal, he sends men to steal it before the Charnetskis can get it to the king of Poland. Adventure, mystery, and self-sacrifice fill this medieval story set in Krakow.

HONORS

The Pigtail of Ah Lee Ben Loo.   John Bennett.   Longmans.

Many original stories in prose and verse, and one brief wordless story, are illustrated with two hundred intriguing and often funny silhouettes. The stories are filled with robust and irreverent humor: King Arthur's Sir Launcelot is called "Sir Launcelot de Id-i-otte"! Most of the stories first appeared in *St. Nicholas Magazine.*

Millions of Cats.   Wanda Gág.   Coward.

A lonely old couple decides to get a cat. Searching for the prettiest one out of a whole hillside filled with cats, the man comes home with "hundreds of cats, thousands of cats, millions and billions and trillions of cats." When the cats fight about who is prettiest, only one is left.

The Boy Who Was. Grace Hallock. Illustrated by Harrie Wood. Dutton.

In 1927 Nino the goatherd shows an artist the wooden figures he has carved of famous Mediterranean people and proceeds to tell their stories, covering more than 3,000 years of history. He begins with tales of Odysseus, Pompeii, and the Crusades and then goes through the nineteenth century, occasionally including himself in the stories.

Clearing Weather. Cornelia Meigs. Illustrated by Frank Dobias. Little, Brown.

It is just after the American Revolution and the economy has not recovered. When young Nicholas Drury takes over his family's shipbuilding business, he struggles hard until the family fortune reverses itself with the successful design, construction, and voyage of the Jocasta, a forerunner of the clipper ship.

Runaway Papoose. Grace Moon. Illustrated by Carl Moon. Doubleday.

Little Nah-tee runs away when outlaw Indians attack her family's camp. Her parents cannot find her and move on with the others. Nah-tee and a young shepherd boy she meets have many adventures as they cross the mesa in search of her parents.

Tod of the Fens. Elinor Whitney. Illustrated by Warwick Goble. Macmillan.

Fifteenth-century Boston, England, is the setting for the amusing tale of Tod, who lives with a band of men just outside of town. Prince Hal, later to become Henry V, roves about the town in various disguises. Tod, realizing what is happening, tells no one and plays along with the game that is afoot.

1928 Award

Gay Neck, the Story of a Pigeon
Dhan Gopal Mukerji   Dutton

Born in Calcutta, Gay Neck has thrilling adventures, first traveling all over India and later working as a carrier pigeon for the Indian Army in France during World War I. Eventually he returns to his young owner in India. Sometimes the story is told by Mukerji and at other times by Gay Neck the pigeon.

HONORS

Downright Dencey. Caroline Snedeker. Illustrated by Maginel Wright Barney. Doubleday.

A Nantucket Quaker community during the War of 1812 provides the background for the story of a young girl named Dencey who first becomes involved with outcast Sammie when she hurls a stone at him. Ashamed, she tries to make amends but Sammie's trust must be won, and that is not easy for Dencey.

The Wonder Smith and His Son. Ella Young. Illustrated by Boris Artzybasheff. Longmans.

Fourteen stories of Gubbaun Saor, a mythological creature of Ireland, have been retold from tales the author heard from English and Gaelic storytellers. The stories capture the lilting cadence of the Irish language and are enhanced by the graphics.

1927 Award

Smoky, the Cowhorse   Will James   Scribner

Born free on the open range, Smoky roams the hills until he is caught and gentled by Clint, a cowboy. Stolen and cruelly treated, Smoky kills his captor and runs as an outlaw. Captured again, he becomes a rodeo horse until once more he meets up with Clint and lives out his life on the range where he was born.

HONOR

No record.

1926 Award

Shen of the Sea   Arthur Bowie Chrisman
Illustrated by Else Hasselriis   Dutton

Sixteen charming and funny original stories are told in traditional folktale style. Most of the stories explain the origins of things like printing, chopsticks, and gunpowder. In several stories, the main character, always reacting the opposite of what is expected, is tricked by the smarter, minor characters.

HONOR

The Voyagers: Being Legends and Romances of Atlantic Discovery. Padraic Colum. Illustrated by Wildred Jones. Macmillan.

Convinced that there is another land far away, Portugal's Prince Henry the Navigator gathers together all those who might know anything about it. In a high tower that overlooks the Atlantic Ocean, stories of legends and voyages are told along with those of the discoveries of Columbus and Ponce de León.

1925 Award

Tales from Silver Lands   Charles Finger
Illustrated by Charles Honore   Doubleday

Nineteen stories that Finger gathered from South American Indian villagers are retold retaining their original flavor. Included are captivating tales of witches, giants, and strange enchantments.

HONORS

Nicholas: A Manhattan Christmas Story.   Annie Carroll Moore.   Illustrated by Jay Van Everen.   Putnam.

Nicholas, eight inches high, is a little boy from Holland who visits New York City for a few months in the 1920s. While there, he attends parties, visits famous landmarks, and learns about the Dutch influence on the city. His first party is at the library, where he is introduced to many book characters.

The Dream Coach.   Anne Parrish.   Macmillan.

The Dream Coach is pulled by one hundred misty horses. Helped by little angels, it travels the night sky dispensing dreams. Four children are introduced in turn, and their fairy-tale-like dreams, often involving inanimate objects that come to life, are shared.

1924 Award

The Dark Frigate   Charles Hawes
Illustrated by Anton Otto Fischer   Little, Brown

A seagoing adventure turns sour when the *Rose of Devon* is seized in mid-ocean by pirates. The vile, ruthless men force nineteen-year-old Philip to be a part of the pirate crew, and the hangman awaits his return to England. Set in the time of King Charles, the story does not romanticize piracy.

HONOR

No record.

1923 Award

The Voyages of Doctor Dolittle
Hugh Lofting   Lippincott

Fun and nonsense reign as Dr. John Dolittle, a medical doctor and naturalist who has the ability to talk to animals, sets sail for Spider Monkey Island. There he unites two tribes, becomes king, and sails home inside the 70,000-year-old great glass sea snail. The story is told by the doctor's nine-and-a-half-year-old assistant.

HONOR

No record.

―――――――――――――――― **1922 Award** ――――――――――――――――

The Story of Mankind
Hendrik Willem van Loon   Liveright

Speaking directly to the reader, the author provides a fascinating picture of history from cave peoples to the present (1920). Ideas, movements, and people are more important than dates, and history is shown as something that builds upon itself.

HONORS

The Old Tobacco Shop: A True Account of What Befell a Little Boy in Search of Adventure. William Bowen. Illustrated by Reginald Birch. Macmillan.

Fred is befriended by the hunchback who runs the tobacco shop. Warned never to smoke the magic tobacco in the porcelain jar shaped like a "Chinaman's head," Fred stays away from it for a long time. One day he falters and suddenly finds himself involved in high adventure on the Spanish Main.

The Golden Fleece and the Heroes Who Lived before Achilles. Padraic Colum. Illustrated by Willy Pogany. Macmillan.

The ancient triumphs and tragedies of the Greek myths are woven through the central story of Jason and his quest for the Golden Fleece. The many stories told by Orpheus to the sailors in the story might be the very ones that the Argonauts heard on their long voyage.

The Great Quest. Charles Hawes. Illustrated by George Varian. Little, Brown.

Twelve-year-old Josiah tells of how his Uncle Seth is tricked by an old friend into selling his shop and buying a ship. Thinking they are going in search of gold, Josiah and his uncle find themselves unwillingly involved in the slave trade and at odds with the crew.

Cedric the Forester. Bernard Marshall. Appleton.

Cedric, son of a thirteenth-century forester, saves Sir Richard's son and is made his squire. Taught to read and fight, Cedric becomes the best crossbowman in England, and, at the Battle of the Eagles, he is knighted.

The Windy Hill. Cornelia Meigs. Macmillan.

A brother and sister visit their older cousin in New England. Their cousin was once jovial but is now mysteriously irritable and preoccupied. A chance meeting with the beeman leads to their hearing stories about their own family's history. As they listen, the two children start to understand the cause of their cousin's anxiety.

The Caldecott Awards

1999–1938

1999 CALDECOTT AWARD

Snowflake Bentley

Jacqueline
Briggs Martin
Illustrated by
Mary Azarian
Houghton Mifflin

SNOWFLAKE BENTLEY

Jacqueline Briggs Martin   *Illustrated by* Mary Azarian

Mary Azarian

Snowflake Bentley takes children back to "the days when farmers worked with ox and sled and cut the dark with lantern light." It introduces Wilson Bentley, a boy who loved snow more than anything in the world and was determined that one day his camera would capture the extraordinary and unique beauty of snowflakes.

Snowflake Bentley has a beautiful and thoughtful design, a poetic and informative text, distinguished illustrations, universal appeal and resonance. Mary Azarian, a Vermont artist who loves snow as much as Wilson Bentley, has created strong and skillfully carved woodcuts that portray sensible, sturdy characters and a timeless rural landscape.

1999 HONOR BOOKS

Duke Ellington
Andrea Davis Pinkney   Illustrated by Brian Pinkney
Hyperion

Brian Pinkney masterfully uses color and movement to introduce today's children to the life and music of Duke Ellington, one of the great composers and jazz musicians of the twentieth century. Pinkney's pictures swirl with bright colors as they rhythmically pull the reader from spread to spread. Accompanied by an equally rhythmic and "jazzy" text, this is a fitting tribute to Ellington.

No, David!
David Shannon   Blue Sky/Scholastic

David, a typically mischievous preschooler, is into everything he shouldn't be and "No, David!" is his mother's constant refrain. Through Shannon's naïve, childlike paintings and his inventive use of line, color and perspective, young David is made real and vulnerable. He is someone to whom readers and listeners of all ages can connect as well as someone for whom a mother's love will be guaranteed.

Snow
Uri Shulevitz   Farrar Straus Giroux

Snow is a magical picture book that captures in ink and watercolor washes the excitement of a small boy and his dog who, despite adult naysayers, steadfastly believe that snow is coming. Though the radio, weather forecasters, and every adult they encounter refuse to see the snow—even as it covers them—boy and dog relish every moment, delighting in the whimsical changes it brings to their town.

Tibet: Through the Red Box
Peter Sís   Frances Foster Books/Farrar Straus Giroux

Through detailed art and lyrical text, Sís takes us on a literal, spiritual, and symbolic journey through time and memory to his own childhood, his separation from a father far away in Tibet and finally their reunion. The detailed art pulls the reader into real and fanciful stories springing from the diary found in the old red lacquered box.

1998 Awards

Rapunzel
Paul O. Zelinsky Dutton

Zelinsky retells the story based on the familiar Grimm's folktale as well as earlier French and Italian sources. The detailed oil paintings are inspired by Renaissance Masters' paintings.

HONORS

The Gardener. Sarah Stewart. Illustrated by David Small. Farrar.

Illustrations, combined with letters home, tell the story of Lydia Grace Finch, a young Depression-era heroine, who transforms her curmudgeonly uncle and his dreary urban neighborhood with her rooftop garden.

Harlem. Walter Dean Myers. Illustrated by Christopher Myers. Scholastic.

Christopher Myers uses ink, gouache, and cut-paper collage to interpret his father's ode to Harlem. A kaleidoscope of words and images leads the reader on a musical journey filled with sass and swing.

There Was an Old Lady Who Swallowed a Fly. Simms Taback. Viking.

The popular American folk song of the old woman with an insatiable taste for life is served up in a fresh presentation. The reader is treated to an insider's view of her progressively excessive appetite through expanding die-cut peepholes to the inevitable climax.

1997 Awards

Golem David Wisniewski Clarion

The Jews in sixteenth-century Prague turn to their rabbi during time of trouble. The Golem, created to protect the Jews, reflects the themes of power and redemption. How the rabbi deals with the soulless clay giant is a tale that is detailed through intricate paper-cuts.

HONORS

Hush! A Thai Lullaby. Minfong Ho. Illustrated by Holly Meade.
Melanie Kroupa/Orchard.

A strong visual narrative tells the story of a mother who warns a crying mosquito, a leaping frog, and a swinging monkey not to waken her sleeping child. This is a gentle, cumulative bedtime story, sure to please and settle down children.

The Graphic Alphabet. David Pelletier. Edited by Neal Porter. Orchard.

This alphabet book uses computer imagery laced with wit and humor to help young children learn the letters. Each letter is not only represented by a word, image, or concept but also *is* the word, image, or concept. Crisp imagery is combined with meticulous design.

The Paperboy. Dav Pilkey. Jackson/Orchard.

A boy wakes in the darkness, bundles his newspapers, and accompanied by his faithful dog delivers the daily papers to the still, dark houses. Carefully balanced compositions and a restrained but rich palette give this story tremendous visual appeal.

Starry Messenger. Peter Sís. Frances Foster Books/Farrar Straus Giroux.

Galileo Galilei's story is illustrated in a style that evokes Renaissance art, architecture, and cartography. The events of his everyday life, the struggles and successes, are captured through detailed attention on each page, which brings to life the world on the verge of discovery.

1996 Award

Officer Buckle and Gloria Peggy Rathmann Putnam

Police dog Gloria's irreverent acrobatics behind Safety Officer Buckle's back contrast with the officer's straight-laced safety tips to school audiences. Original, lively, and energetic art leads the readers through a story of cooperation and friendship. Watercolor and ink illustrations employ brilliant colors that, combined with a creative use of white space, engage the reader in the humor and warmth of this stellar performance.

HONORS

Alphabet City. Stephen T. Johnson. Viking.

Photorealistic paintings of urban environment present an imaginative variety of views and perspectives, textures, and light. Each painting stands alone as a handsome, balanced piece. Together they are an inspiring exercise in seeing patterns and art in everyday things.

Zin! Zin! Zin! a Violin. Lloyd Moss. Illustrated by Marjorie Priceman. Simon & Schuster.

This exuberant introduction to the orchestra is a true celebration of music. The sense of visual musicality is enhanced by warm, changing background colors. The musicians themselves are far from static, and the text has rhythm and punch, changing size and moving across the pages in swoops and swirls to reflect the flow of music.

The Faithful Friend. Robert D. San Souci. Illustrated by Brian Pinkney. Simon & Schuster.

Pinkney's distinctive illustrations evoke the mystery, magic, and romance in San Souci's retelling of this West Indian folktale. The unique scratchboard style, enhanced by vivid oil colors, is a superb match for this atmospheric story in which the main characters confront and ultimately overcome the dark forces of evil.

Tops & Bottoms. Adapted and illustrated by Janet Stevens. Harcourt.

Sleepy, sprawling bear is outwitted by the wily hare, who succeeds in feeding his numerous offspring with abundant vegetable harvests. Handmade vegetable paper and a masterful use of mixed media contribute to this zesty, organic combination of story and illustration.

1995 Award

Smoky Night
Eve Bunting   Illustrated by David Diaz   Harcourt

Inspired by the Los Angeles riots, *Smoky Night* relates the happenings of a night of urban rioting from a child's perspective. With thickly textured, expressionistic acrylic paintings set against mixed-media collages, Diaz creates dramatic, groundbreaking illustrations of the night's events. Both language and illustration convey the universal importance of human interaction through the personal story of one little boy and his cat.

HONORS

Swamp Angel. Anne Issacs. Illustrated by Paul O. Zelinsky. Dutton.

In this original tall tale, Angelica Longrider, known as Swamp Angel, wrestles the huge bear Thundering Tarnation to save the winter supplies of settlers in Tennessee. With his whimsical illustrations, Paul O. Zelinsky has created a memorable heroine with the grit and gusto of a Paul Bunyan. Primitive-style oil paintings on cherry, maple, and birch veneers capture the folksy feel of life in nineteenth-century Tennessee.

John Henry. Julius Lester. Illustrated by Jerry Pinkney. Dial.

Pinkney's earthy, craggy pencil and watercolor illustrations capture both the power and the humanity of this African-American folk-hero. Masterful use of light and shadow portray the strength and mass of the Allegheny mountains, which match the magnitude of John Henry, while delicate shading and mottled color suggest the detail of a realistic natural setting enlivened with touches of whimsy.

Time Flies. Eric Rohmann. Crown.

Stunning oil paintings in this wordless picture book dramatically portray a bird's flight though a museum display into the age of the living dinosaurs, where it encounters creatures vastly larger than itself. Rohmann uses rich, realistic shading; texture; and varying perspectives to create the bird's fanciful journey back to the time of its primitive ancestors.

1994 Award

Grandfather's Journey
Allen Say   Edited by Walter Lorraine   Houghton

Grandfather's Journey eloquently portrays a Japanese immigrant's travels to a new land. Exquisite watercolors portray vast landscapes along with intimate family portraits that communicate hope, dignity, sadness, and love. Say powerfully connects the personal and the universal to create a rare harmony of longing and belonging.

HONORS

Peppe the Lamplighter.   Illustrated by Ted Lewin, written by Elisa Bartone.   Lothrop.

Lewin vividly captures the bustling market scenes, bleak tenement rooms, and the lamplit streets of turn-of-the-century New York's Little Italy. Dramatic watercolors portray young Peppe's struggle to help support his immigrant family and to win his father's respect.

In the Small, Small Pond.   Denise Fleming.   Holt.

Bright colors and lively language describe the cycle of pond life. Rhyming alliterative text and vibrant illustrations are filled with movement and fun in a joyous celebration of the natural world. Fleming created the illustration by pouring colored pulp through hand-cut stencils.

Owen.   Kevin Henkes.   Greenwillow.

A preschooler mouse, Owen, and his concerned parents confront a classic childhood drama: releasing the trusty, fuzzy blanket. Confident economical line and inspired layout convey Owen's spirited tenacity as he dances toward greater independence.

Raven: A Trickster Tale from the Pacific Northwest.   Gerald McDermott. Harcourt.

McDermott reshapes the familiar trickster tale from the Pacific Northwest in which Raven steals light from the Sky Chief and brings it to people. Raven's spirit world is boldly colored and hard-edged, a strong graphic contrast to the soft watercolor background of the real Northwest landscape.

Yo! Yes?   Chris Raschka.   Edited by Richard Jackson.   Orchard.

Through bold, original use of line and angle, color and space, Raschka celebrates friendship and offers a timeless message about taking risks. The brief, rhythmic text invites enthusiastic sharing.

1993 Award

Mirette on the High Wire
Emily Arnold McCully   Putnam

Emily Arnold McCully's vivid impressionistic watercolors bring nineteenth-century Paris to life with the story of Mirette, a spirited, risk-taking little girl. Mirette enables the former high-wire star Bellini to conquer his fear while achieving her own dream. Light, color, line, and movement in these animated and bold illustrations are in perfect balance with the text.

HONORS

The Stinky Cheese Man & Other Fairly Stupid Tales. Illustrated by Lane Smith, written by Jon Scieszka. Viking.

> The Little Red Hen talks in red letters and the giant talks in capitals in this irreverent retelling of the gingerbread man and other time-honored tales. The avant-garde art ("rendered in oil and vinegar" according to the book note) lampoons twentieth-century art in the process. Interdependence of words, visual images, and even the process of book design and publication extract every possible laugh in this outrageous collaboration.

Working Cotton. Illustrated by Carole Byard, written by Sherley Anne Williams. Harcourt.

> Carole Byard's dramatic paintings portray the dignity of hard work and the strength of family relationships that are part of this migrant family's life. From the first glimpses of a streaky dawn to the red twilight, powerful, glowing portraits and landscapes poignantly complement the child's poetic depiction of the long workday.

Seven Blind Mice. Ed Young. Philomel Books.

> In this successful reinterpretation of the Indian fable of the blind man and the elephant, deceptively simple text integrates concepts of color, numbers, and days of the week with visual irony. Contrasting textured paper heightens the bold color and strong composition, while white typeface against a glossy background and marbleized endpapers add to the excellent design.

1992 Award

Tuesday
David Wiesner   Clarion Books

Flying frogs on lily pads create mischief as they move from the fen to a small town on a Tuesday evening. The story ends with a comic twist suggesting more fantastic flights for the following Tuesday. Wiesner's watercolor illustrations show masterful use of light and dark, alternating perspectives, and variation in page design in this nine-word book.

HONOR

Tar Beach. Faith Ringgold. Crown Publishers, Inc., a Random House Co.

Child Cassie flies high above New York City in the 1930s, high above the quilt squares that ground each page, high above the busyness and conflict of everyday life, from family rooftop picnics to daddy's construction work. Acrylic paintings on canvas paper form the basis of this visual feast celebrating the act of transformation, while the quilt form represents an historically important African-American communication medium.

1991 Award

Black and White
David Macaulay   Houghton

Macaulay interweaves fantasy and reality in a tale of parents, trains, and cows. The author recommends careful inspection of words and pictures to both minimize and enhance confusion.

HONORS

Puss in Boots. Fred Marcellino. di Capua/Farrar.

Large pale type and golden-toned paintings work brilliantly together providing an elegant regal look to the familiar fairy tale of Puss. With varied perspectives and points of view, Marcellino re-creates the French court and countryside to ingenious, often droll, effect.

"More, More, More," Said the Baby: 3 Love Stories. Vera B. Williams. Greenwillow.

Brightly framed gouache paintings reflect each child's sense of security and joy as a loving adult "catches" that baby up. This creative use of color, shape, and rhythm marks a unique and distinctive celebration of family life.

1990 Award

Lon Po Po: A Red-Riding Hood Story from China
Ed Young   Philomel

Suspense and drama are lightened with bits of humor as the wolf Lon Po Po tries to trick three children into letting him into their house. Though he succeeds, the children quickly turn the tables on the wily animal. The artist uses vivid watercolors and pastels to create dramatic panel pictures.

HONORS

Color Zoo. Lois Ehlert. Lippincott.

Vibrant colors and overlays of geometric-shaped cutouts in heavy paper combine to create expressive animal faces. The text is simply a one-word identification of the shape or animal. All of the action is in the creative paper engineering.

Hershel and the Hanukkah Goblins. Eric Kimmel. Illustrated by
Trina Schart Hyman. Holiday House.

> Eight goblins haunt the old synagogue, preventing the villagers from cele-
> brating Hanukkah until Hershel arrives to outwit all of the creatures. The
> dark illustrations are charged with energy as they show the imaginatively
> wicked goblins trying to frighten Hershel away.

Bill Peet: An Autobiography. Bill Peet. Houghton.

> From the time he learned to manipulate a crayon, drawing has been a con-
> suming passion for Bill Peet. He tells how that passion affected his life, from
> childhood, through his work at the Disney Studios, to his life as an author.
> Using his usual artistic style, Peet has filled his autobiography with new
> black-and-white illustrations.

The Talking Eggs. Robert D. San Souci. Illustrated by Jerry Pinkney. Dial.

> Running away from her angry mother and spoiled sister, Blanche is be-
> friended by a strange old woman who owns a cow with two heads and chick-
> ens that lay talking eggs. The eerie and suspenseful black folktale is filled
> with watercolor pictures of deep woods and strange sights.

1989 Award

Song and Dance Man   Karen Ackerman
Illustrated by Stephen Gammell   Knopf

When his grandchildren come to visit, Grandpa whisks them up to the attic,
where he performs an exciting vaudeville routine. The colored-pencil
sketches are alive with movement and drama.

HONORS

Mirandy and Brother Wind. Patricia C. McKissack. Illustrated by
Jerry Pinkney. Knopf.

> A sparkling, energetic Mirandy vows to dance with the wind at her first cake-
> walk—but to do that, she must catch it first. Lush, expansive illustrations of
> the rural South capture the vigor and imagination of the story.

Goldilocks and the Three Bears. Illustrated by James Marshall. Dial.

> The antithesis of the typical sweet, demure Goldilocks, this little girl with her
> bouncing golden ringlets is brash, irreverent, and captivating. Set in the pres-
> ent day, the briefly told nursery story abounds with color, humor, and wit.

The Boy of the Three-Year Nap. Diane Snyder. Illustrated by Allen Say.
Houghton.

> Taro has earned his nickname because of his laziness and penchant for sleep-
> ing. When he turns trickster to stop his industrious mother's nagging, she in
> turn outwits him. The handsome pictures are noticeably influenced by eigh-
> teenth-century Japanese woodcuts and reflect the culture of the land where
> this folktale originated.

Free Fall. Illustrated by David Wiesner. Lothrop.

In a book made more powerful because it has no woods to stifle the imagination, a boy falls asleep and dreams of fantastic adventures. In this visual story, the objects around the boy evolve from one thing into another and then back to their original shapes.

1988 Award

Owl Moon
Jane Yolen   Illustrated by John Schoenherr   Philomel

Late one quiet winter's night, a little girl and her father go owling, watching and listening for the signs that say a great horned owl is nearby. Blue-toned color washes and simple landscapes create a frosty, magical night perfect for owl watching.

HONOR

Mufaro's Beautiful Daughters: An African Tale. John Steptoe. Lothrop.

Of the two sisters, one kind and good, the other mean and deceitful, only one will be chosen to marry the king. Dramatic yet realistic paintings in lush, jewel-toned colors illustrate this folktale from Zimbabwe.

1987 Award

Hey, Al   Arthur Yorinks
Illustrated by Richard Egielski   Farrar

Janitor Al and his dog are swept away from their apparently humdrum lives by a huge bird that takes them to what at first seems like paradise. Full-color illustrations provide florid scenes of that paradise.

HONORS

The Village of Round and Square Houses. Ann Grifalconi. Little, Brown.

Pastel drawings are used to illustrate the story of the remote Cameron village of Tos where the women live in the round houses and the men live in the square ones so that each has a place to be together and a place to be apart.

Alphabatics. Suse MacDonald. Bradbury.

Brightly colored letters of the alphabet become acrobats as they twist and turn until they become the objects that represent the letters: A becomes an ark, J becomes a jack-in-the-box, S becomes a swan.

Rumpelstiltskin. Paul O. Zelinsky. Dutton.

When the proud father tells the king that his daughter can spin straw into gold, it is the tiny Rumpelstiltskin who actually does the spinning—for the price of the first-born child. Golden-toned, full-color oil paintings in medieval style retell this tale based on an early Brothers Grimm version.

--- **1986 Award** ---

The Polar Express
Chris Van Allsburg   Houghton

Dark, brooding illustrations with unusual perspectives set the mood for a magical and poignant train ride. It is Christmas Eve when the young boy boards the train for a trip to the North Pole. There he receives a special gift from Santa Claus.

HONORS

The Relatives Came. Cynthia Rylant.   Illustrated by Stephen Gammell. Bradbury.

What a marvelous time is had when all the relatives come from Virginia for a visit! They crowd into the house, where there is much loving and hugging and breathing to do together! The pictures nearly bounce off the pages with all the love and happiness in this book.

King Bidgood's in the Bathtub. Audrey Wood.   Illustrated by Don Wood. Harcourt.

When the court is in a dither because the king refuses to get out of the bathtub, only the young page knows what to do. Illustrations reminiscent of an opera stage setting show off the full glory of the court scenes.

--- **1985 Award** ---

Saint George and the Dragon
Retold by Margaret Hodges
Illustrated by Trina Schart Hyman   Little, Brown

Lady Una and George, a knight of the Red Cross, must find and battle the terrible dragon that ruins the land. Hyman's illustrations tell the story dramatically, and the reader seems to look at the scenes through an iron-encased window.

HONORS

Hansel and Gretel. Retold by Rika Lesser.   Illustrated by Paul O. Zelinsky. Dodd.

In this book translated from one of the less-embellished versions of the classic Brothers Grimm story, the artwork dominates. Sometimes imitating sixteenth- and seventeenth-century Flemish art, sometimes adopting a romantic nineteenth-century style, the paintings are rich in color and detail.

The Story of Jumping Mouse. Retold and illustrated by John Steptoe. Lothrop.

Large, expressive pencil drawings help tell the tale of a field mouse's search for the Far-Off Land. Armed with courage and hope, the mouse overcomes many obstacles until it is transformed into an eagle. The text is freely adapted from an unidentified Native American "why" story.

Have You Seen My Duckling? Nancy Tafuri. Greenwillow.
In this almost wordless book, a duck asks the creatures of the pond if they have seen her lost duckling. Bright, clear illustrations show the adventuresome duckling, who is always seen a little hidden from but close to his mother.

1984 Award

The Glorious Flight: Across the Channel with Louis Blériot
Alice and Martin Provensen   Viking

Once he sees a flying machine, Louis Blériot becomes passionately interested in building his own machine and is successful on his eleventh attempt. Based on a true incident in France in the early 1900s, the biography is illustrated with pictures of shifting perspectives and touches of humor and views of a family growing older.

HONORS

Ten, Nine, Eight. Molly Bang. Greenwillow.
Bedtime becomes a favorite time as the countdown begins. In a lulling rhyme, all of the things in a little girl's room are counted. The quiet time shared between father and daughter is illustrated with warm colors.

Little Red Riding Hood. Retold and illustrated by Trina Schart Hyman. Holiday.
The familiar story of the little girl who goes to visit her grandmother subtly warns children not to talk to strangers. The detailed illustrations seem to place the setting of the story in New England.

1983 Award

Shadow   Blaise Cendrars
Translated and illustrated by Marcia Brown   Scribner

Translated from the French poet Blaise Cendrars' work, this symbolic mood piece reflects stories told by African storytellers and shamans around a nighttime fire. Rich colors with black cutout accents create the visual image of the prowling, dancing, mute shadow.

HONORS

When I Was Young in the Mountains. Cynthia Rylant. Illustrated by Diane Goode. Dutton.
The author affectionately recalls a childhood spent with her family in the Appalachian Mountains of West Virginia. Warm family scenes are filled with friendly, happy people. Many of the illustrations drift off into the mountain mist and bring a peacefulness to the recalled pleasures.

A Chair for My Mother.   Vera B. Williams.   Greenwillow.

After a fire destroys their home, a little girl, her waitress mother, and the girl's grandmother move into an apartment. They start saving all their coins for a big, comfortable chair for Mama and Grandma. The watercolor paintings have a suitably childlike look.

1982 Award

Jumanji
Chris Van Allsburg   Houghton

Looking for something to do on a boring afternoon, Peter and Judy decide to try the strange board game they find in the park. Boredom vanishes as every space on which they land comes to life. Meticulously crafted black-and-white illustrations bring the game alive.

HONORS

Where the Buffaloes Begin.   Olaf Baker.   Illustrated by Stephen Gammell. Warne.

Majestic, haunting, and moody gray-toned illustrations show Little Wolf on his journey to the sacred place where buffaloes are said to originate. The rich prose was first published in *St. Nicholas Magazine* in 1915.

On Market Street.   Arnold Lobel.   Illustrated by Anita Lobel.   Greenwillow.

A nursery rhyme-like verse breaks into a celebration of all the wares—from A to Z—that a little boy purchases on Market Street. The illustrations, based on seventeenth-century French trade engravings, show brightly colored shopkeepers composed of their merchandise.

Outside over There.   Maurice Sendak.   Harper.

When Ida is not focusing her complete attention on her baby sister, the baby is kidnapped by hooded goblins and replaced by a baby made of ice. Elaborate paintings combine romantic and surrealistic effects and are filled with subtleties and symbolism.

A Visit to William Blake's Inn: Poems for Innocent and Experienced Travelers.
Nancy Willard.   Illustrated by Alice and Martin Provensen.   Harcourt.

Lyrical poems written in the spirit of William Blake combine with captivatingly imaginative illustrations that reflect the staidness and the whimsy of the eighteenth century. Nancy Willard also won the 1982 Newbery Award for this book.

--------- **1981 Award** ---------

Fables
Arnold Lobel   Harper

Twenty original, brief, and witty animal fables, each complete with a moral, expose human foibles. Each fable is faced with a full-page painting in soft, rich colors that show the droll animals at the crucial moment of the fable.

HONORS

The Grey Lady and the Strawberry Snatcher.   Molly Bang.   Four Winds.

An old lady who, except for her hands and face, appears as a grey silhouette, buys a basket of strawberries and proceeds home, pursued by a strawberry snatcher. Interesting colors and textures are effectively combined with negative grey shapes in this vivid visual hide-and-seek game.

Truck.   Donald Crews.   Greenwillow.

Bright colors and geometric shapes roll across the pages as a truck carries a cargo of tricycles to its destination. There is no text. From the loading dock, through intricate highway systems, past road signs, to a truck stop, in clear and stormy weather, the big red truck moves its precious cargo across the country.

Mice Twice.   Joseph Low.   McElderry/Atheneum.

Cat is very hungry and wants a nice tender mouse to eat, so he invites Mouse to dinner. Things escalate until even Lion and Crocodile are involved. It is Wasp who settles things in this funny tale that is enhanced through whimsical drawings.

The Bremen-Town Musicians.   Retold and illustrated by Ilse Plume. Doubleday.

Four animals, all unwanted, set out together to become musicians but instead end up outwitting a band of robbers. The Brothers Grimm tale is illustrated with glowing, subdued colors and rounded shapes.

--------- **1980 Award** ---------

Ox-Cart Man
Donald Hall   Illustrated by Barbara Cooney   Viking

Clean, uncluttered paintings capture the flavor of nineteenth-century New England as a family's day-to-day life is mandated by the changing season. There is a strong sense of the passage of time and rhythm of life in this book.

HONORS

Ben's Trumpet.   Rachel Isadora.   Greenwillow.

The mood, sounds, and rhythms of jazz pulsate through the illustrations as Ben sits on the fire escape and blows his imaginary trumpet to the jazz sounds eminating from the Zig Zig Jazz Club. Set in the twenties and illustrated with dynamic black-and-white drawings, this is the story of one boy's dream coming true

The Treasure. Uri Shulevitz. Farrar.

A poor man dreams that he must go to the castle bridge and wait for something that will turn about his fortunes. Traveling far to get there, he learns that the treasure is under his own stove. Illustrations with softly glowing colors and a striking use of light depict traditional eastern European villages and countrysides.

The Garden of Abdul Gasazi. Chris Van Allsburg. Houghton.

Illusion and reality become blurred when the unruly dog the boy has been tending runs away into the secret, foreboding garden of a retired magician. The visual perspectives and the play of light on the gray pencil drawings create an eerie, mysterious feeling.

1979 Award

The Girl Who Loved Wild Horses
Paul Goble   Bradbury

The kinship is so strong between a Plains Indian girl and the horses she has lived with since becoming lost in a storm, that eventually she becomes one of them. Sharp, brilliantly colored paintings sweep across the pages and are in perfect harmony with the story.

HONORS

Freight Train. Donald Crews. Greenwillow.

Large pictures of the different freight cars are identified by name and by color. Soon the train begins to move into a blur of colors as it swiftly goes on its way.

The Way to Start a Day. Byrd Baylor. Illustrated by Peter Parnall. Scribner.

A vibrant sunflower yellow and other colors blend with crisp, black lines to make effective use of symbolism in celebration of the sun. Poetic prose tells how cultures throughout the ages have sung to the new day's sun to honor it.

1978 Award

Noah's Ark
Peter Spier   Doubleday

The only text is the seventeenth-century Dutch poem, "The Flood," by Jacobus Revius, that opens the book. The rest of the book is a visual interpretation of Noah and his unbelievably difficult task of tending the animals on the ark. Careful details and softly hued watercolors depict the story with reverence, humor, and delight.

HONORS

Castle. David Macaulay. Houghton.

Macaulay traces in text and drawings the step-by-step construction of a fictitious thirteenth-century English castle in Wales from its conception to its baptism by fire—a direct attack by hundreds of Welsh soldiers. The complex engineering task is generously illustrated with detailed black-and-white line drawings and diagrams.

It Could Always Be Worse. Retold and illustrated by Margot Zemach. Farrar.

Crowded into one room with his mother, wife, and six children, a man goes to the rabbi for help. The rabbi's answer is to bring one animal after another to live in the house. Dynamic, earth-toned paintings with an eastern European look capture the humor of the rabbi's good advice.

1977 Award

Ashanti to Zulu: African Traditions Margaret Musgrove Illustrated by Leo and Diane Dillon Dial

Twenty-six different African tribal traditions and customs are introduced using the English alphabet as the vehicle. A border on each page frames the text and illustrations, where glowing colors mix with rich browns. The attention to authentic detail in each painting is remarkable.

HONORS

Hawk, I'm Your Brother. Byrd Baylor. Illustrated by Peter Parnall. Scribner.

In a gentle story told in simple, poetic prose, a young Native American boy wants desperately to fly like a hawk. Spacious, clean, panoramic line drawings convey the yearning of the boy and the power of the hawk.

Fish for Supper. M. B. Goffstein. Dial.

This quiet story chronicles the simple daily routine of Grandma, whose life centers around fishing. The black-and-white line drawings are centered in a square border of white space.

The Contest. Retold and illustrated by Nonny Hogrogian. Greenwillow.

Realizing that they are both engaged to the same woman and each unwilling to give her up, two robbers compare their cleverness in thievery to see who deserves her. Large, colorful illustrations capture the flavor of the Armenian culture in this humorous folktale.

The Golem. Beverly Brodsky McDermott. Lippincott.

The somber Jewish legend of the Golem, a creature created from clay that becomes more powerful and terrible than the evil he was made to destroy, is re-created with high visual drama. Striking paintings, vibrant with deep, rich colors, are filled with symbolism and massive shapes.

The Amazing Bone. William Steig. Farrar.

On her way home from school, hapless heroine Pearl Pig finds an amazing talking bone. When the delectable piglet is waylaid by a debonair fox, the amazing bone saves Pearl. Sunny, fresh, springtime landscapes provide the background for the well-dressed characters.

1976 Award

Why Mosquitoes Buzz in People's Ears
Retold by Verna Aardema
Illustrated by Leo and Diane Dillon   Dial

Mosquito tells Iguana a tall tale about yams that annoys Iguana so much that he puts sticks in his ears so he cannot hear such things. Thus begins a chain reaction tale of the West African jungle. Illustrations show highly stylized animals.

HONORS

The Desert Is Theirs. Byrd Baylor. Illustrated by Peter Parnall. Scribner.

A spare, lyrical text tells of the relationship of the Papagos people to their environment—"we share . . . we only share." The paintings are dramatic and are reminiscent of the layers of colors found in sand paintings.

Strega Nona. Tomie de Paola. Prentice-Hall.

Strega Nona leaves Big Anthony alone with her magic pasta pot after telling him never to touch it. It is not long before he does, and pasta literally flows through the town. Characters in medieval costumes of pastel, jewel-like colors add to the humor of the story.

1975 Award

Arrow to the Sun
Gerald McDermott   Viking

The son of the Lord of the Sun sets out to find his father in this adaptation of a Pueblo legend. On his way, he undergoes four trials to prove his relationship to the Sun. The stylized, strong geometric art vividly portrays the desert and its intense sun colors.

HONOR

Jambo Means Hello. Muriel Feelings. Illustrated by Tom Feelings. Dial.

Letters of the alphabet are represented by words of the Swahili language. A brief explanation of the word includes cultural information of East African countries. Beautiful full-page illustrations further depict the cultures.

1974 Award

Duffy and the Devil
Retold by Harve Zemach
Illustrated by Margot Zemach   Farrar

The Cornish version of Rumpelstiltskin has delightful twists. When the maid guesses the devil's name, everything that he has sewn turns to ashes. Lightly colored illustrations treat the story with grand humor, and at the instant the name is guessed, the Squire is left standing in the fields, naked except for hat and shoes.

HONORS

Three Jovial Huntsmen. Susan Jeffers. Bradbury.

The three jovial huntsmen go a-hunting on St. David's day and find nothing they want. But lurking in the beautifully drawn forests, many animals are seen keeping a close watch on the huntsmen.

Cathedral. David Macaulay. Houghton.

The single-mindedness and spirit of the people and their step-by-step construction of an imaginary medieval cathedral are meticulously recorded as the author-illustrator celebrates the lives and art of the craftsmen who built the magnificent Gothic cathedrals.

1973 Award

The Funny Little Woman   Retold by Arlene Mosel
Illustrated by Blair Lent   Dutton

A little woman pursues a rice dumpling and is led into the underground world of the wicked Oni. Her escape proves she is a funny little woman. Illustrations convey the mystery and humor of the strange world of the Oni as well as the dignity of this Japanese folktale.

HONORS

Hosie's Alphabet. Hosea, Tobias and Lisa Baskin. Illustrated by Leonard Baskin. Viking.

From the bumptious baboon, to the primordial protozoa, right down to the "ruminating zebu," the artist presents an alphabet bestiary of ever-changing format where spiders' legs stretch across the page and dashes of watercolor become the eagle. This work is highly imaginative.

When Clay Sings. Byrd Baylor. Illustrated by Tom Bahti. Scribner.

Illustrated with the designs found on prehistoric pottery from the American Southwest, this tribute to artifacts and those who used them evokes a reverence for an ancient way of life. The earth tones and prehistoric designs dignify the word images of the poetic text.

Snow-White and the Seven Dwarfs. A Tale from the Brothers Grimm. Translated by Randall Jarrell. Illustrated by Nancy Ekholm Burkert. Farrar.

Strongly detailed illustrations in beautiful, soft colors evoke the sweeping, medieval, magical romance of fairy tales. Randall Jarrell translated the Brothers Grimm story of the beautiful girl, the wicked, malicious step-mother, and the sturdy, somber dwarfs.

Anansi the Spider: A Tale from the Ashanti. Adapted and illustrated by Gerald McDermott. Holt.

The moon is in the sky because Anansi, the great African folklore hero, could not decide which of his six sons should have it. Bright, geometric designs, bold, stylized animals, and rhythmic speech patterns are based on the Ashanti culture.

1972 Award

One Fine Day
Retold and illustrated by Nonny Hogrogian   Macmillan

Punished by having his tail cut off when he drank all the milk in an old woman's pail, the fox pleads to have it sewn back on so his friends won't make fun of him. The old woman agrees to do it, but only after he has returned her milk. The subdued and uncluttered pictures reflect the humorous cumulative action of the Armenian tale.

HONORS

If All the Seas Were One Sea. Janina Domanska. Macmillan.

An old nursery rhyme, its rise-and-fall rhythmic text reminiscent of the action of ocean waves, is treated to splendid etchings boldly filled with swirling, geometric lines of clear colors. The many shapes of each etching make a whole picture and provide the rhyme with even more momentum.

Moja Means One: Swahili Counting Book. Muriel Feelings. Illustrated by Tom Feelings. Dial.

Numbers from one to ten are represented by words in the Swahili language. Handsome, muted-gray double-page spread paintings depict scenes from Africa and relate to the illustrative sentences.

Hildilid's Night. Cheli Duran Ryan. Illustrated by Arnold Lobel. Macmillan.

Hildilid hates the night and the creatures of it. She does everything she can to chase the night away. Pen-and-ink drawings composed of thousands of tiny lines add a moonlit quality to the pages. Only at the end, with the approach of dawn, does yellow come into the picture.

1971 Award

A Story A Story
Retold and illustrated by Gail E. Haley   Atheneum

Kwaku Ananse, the great African spider man, completes three almost impossible tasks to win the Sky God's box of stories to tell throughout the world. The woodcut illustrations use African designs.

HONORS

Frog and Toad Are Friends. Arnold Lobel. Harper.

In five affectionate and funny stories, best friends Frog and Toad share simple adventures and experiences. They welcome spring, find a lost button, tell stories, and enjoy being friends. The expressive and droll illustrations are in gray, frog green, and toad brown.

In the Night Kitchen. Maurice Sendak. Harper.

Falling through the night and out of his clothes, Mickey lands in cake batter in the night kitchen. From there he goes to the dough, builds an airplane of it, and flies to the Milky Way. The dream-fantasy is carried out in a chanting rhyme and is illustrated with an adaptation of comic book art.

The Angry Moon. Retold by William Sleator. Illustrated by Blair Lent. Atlantic.

A legend of the peoples of Alaska is retold with vigor, using lavish, full-color illustrations that elaborate on original Tlingit motifs. When Lapowinsa mocks the moon, she is taken into the sky country. Her friend must overcome many obstacles before he is able to rescue her.

1970 Award

Sylvester and the Magic Pebble
William Steig   Windmill

A collector of pebbles, Sylvester the donkey finds a magic one that grants wishes. Caught by a lion, Sylvester panics and wishes himself to be a rock. Full-color pictures show the seasonal changes and colorful characters of the story and extend its concern and gentle humor.

HONORS

Goggles! Ezra Jack Keats. Macmillan.

While showing off the motorcycle goggles he has found, Peter is accosted by neighborhood bullies. Proving that smart moves are more powerful than brute strength, Peter and his friends outwit the older boys. Rich, dark, brooding colors of paint and collage are lightened with vibrant colors in illustrations that reflect the urban setting.

Alexander and the Wind-Up Mouse. Leo Lionni. Pantheon.
Alexander, an unappreciated house mouse, envies Willy the windup mouse
because everyone loves and coddles him. After asking the wizard lizard to
change him into a windup mouse, Alexander has a change of heart. Large,
bold collages enhance the simply told story.

Pop Corn and Ma Goodness. Edna Mitchell Preston. Illustrated by
Robert Andrew Parker. Viking.
With all the gaiety and drama of a folk song, this original story is told in nonsense verse. Ma Goodness and Pop Corn meet, fall in love, marry, build a
house and a farm, have children, and enjoy the good life on their "prippitty
proppetty." Watercolor pictures have a haphazard look that adds to the rol-
licking fun.

Thy Friend, Obadiah. Brinton Turkle. Viking.
His large Quaker family teases young Obadiah because a sea gull has taken a
liking to him and follows him everywhere. The drawings are warm and gentle and vary greatly in perspective. When the sea gull fails to be seen for several days, Obadiah finds that what he thought was a nuisance is really a
friend.

The Judge: An Untrue Tale. Harve Zemach. Illustrated by Margot Zemach.
Farrar.
Prisoner after prisoner excitedly tells the Judge about the horrible thing that
is on its way. The no-nonsense Judge throws them all in jail. When the horrible thing comes, poetic justice is done. Illustrated in watercolors and line
drawings, the robust, pinkish characters tell their cumulative rhyming tale.

––––––––––––––––––––––––– **1969 Award** –––––––––––––––––––––––––

The Fool of the World and the Flying Ship
Retold by Arthur Ransome
Illustrated by Uri Shulevitz   Farrar

Line drawings and watercolors in bright, glowing, jewel-toned colors show
the magnificent flying ship and the landscapes and onion domes of Russia.
In this old Russian tale, the scorned and foolish younger son of peasants
overcomes tremendous obstacles and wins the hand of the czar's daughter.

HONOR

Why the Sun and the Moon Live in the Sky. Elphinstone Dayrell.
Illustrated by Blair Lent. Houghton.
Long ago, so the Nigerian folktale says, the Sun and Water were friends and
lived on Earth together. When Sun invites Water to visit, the resulting flood
forces them into the sky. Elaborately stylized African motifs and traditional
patterns are used throughout the book.

1968 Award

Drummer Hoff   Barbara Emberley
Illustrated by Ed Emberley   Prentice-Hall

"Private Parridge brought the carriage," begins the cumulative text that leads to "Drummer Hoff fired it off" and a big "Kahbahbloom." Woodcuts show vibrantly colored old-fashioned military figures.

HONORS

Frederick.   Leo Lionni.   Pantheon.

The other field mice scurry to gather food for winter while Frederick gathers warm thoughts. In the deep of winter when the food has run out, Frederick is called upon to share his supplies. Collages enhance this story that proves "we do not live by bread alone."

Seashore Story.   Taro Yashima.   Viking.

On an island where "the quietness of ancient times" is felt, visiting children are reminded of the old story of Urashima, a fisherman who saved the life of a turtle. In return, the turtle takes him deep into the ocean to a mythical land. Muted pastel drawings capture the mysticism of the Japanese story.

The Emperor and the Kite.   Jane Yolen.   Illustrated by Ed Young.   World.

Djeow Seow was the smallest and least noticed of the emperor's children. When evil men come and snatch the emperor away, it is Djeow Seow and her kites who rescue him. Intricate paper cuttings provide great beauty and a sense of cultural heritage in this Japanese tale.

1967 Award

Sam, Bangs & Moonshine
Evaline Ness   Holt

Sam, a fisherman's daughter, has a bad habit of making up stories. The little girl learns to distinguish the truth from "moonshine" only after her best friend and her cat nearly meet tragedy. The book's pictures capture Sam's confusion of fact and fancy.

HONOR

One Wide River to Cross.   Adapted by Barbara Emberley.   Illustrated by Ed Emberley.   Prentice-Hall.

The text of an old folk song comes alive on brightly colored pages printed with black woodcuts. Stylized animals come forth one by one, two by two, and so on up to ten in nonsense verse with illustrations of animals that cumulate in groups waiting to board Noah's ark.

1966 Award

Always Room for One More
Sorche Nic Leodhas, pseud. (Leclaire Alger)
Illustrated by Nonny Hogrogian   Holt

A man invites all passersby to share his house with his wife and ten children until the house finally bursts apart. The Scottish folk song is told in lilting verse and illustrated in a subdued, dreamy manner.

HONORS

Just Me. Marie Hall Ets. Viking.

The little boy tries to imitate the hops, walks, and wiggles of the animals on his farm. But when he sees his father, he runs to him as only he can run. Black-and-white drawings have a charming rhythmic expression.

Tom Tit Tot. Retold and illustrated by Evaline Ness. Scribner.

In this English variant of Rumpelstiltskin, the heroine is a comic, homespun character. Woodcuts executed in brown, gold, black, and aqua capture the broad humor and Elizabethan tone of the story.

Hide and Seek Fog. Alvin Tresselt. Illustrated by Roger Duvoisin. Lothrop.

As thick fog settles down for a stay, the lobstermen cannot put out to sea, the vacationers grumble because they cannot do anything, and the children frolic and play hide-and-seek. Pictures and text describe how life becomes transformed in a dense, wet, lingering fog on the Atlantic seacoast.

1965 Award

May I Bring a Friend?
Written by Beatrice Schenk de Regniers
Illustrated by Beni Montresor   Atheneum

Invited to tea by the king and queen each day of one week, the child quite naturally asks if he can bring a friend with him. Each day he brings animals from the zoo, and not all are well behaved! In rhymed text and creative illustrations reminiscent of stage settings, the absurd story is told.

HONORS

A Pocketful of Cricket. Rebecca Caudill. Illustrated by Evaline Ness. Holt.

One day a boy who delights in the countryside finds a cricket and takes it home for a pet. An understanding teacher shows him how to share his special love of the cricket with the whole class. Pictures portray the inquisitiveness of a young farm boy.

The Wave. Margaret Hodges. Illustrated by Blair Lent. Houghton.

Giisan, the wise and respected old man of the Japanese village, must act quickly to warn the villagers that they are in great danger. The relentlessness of the tidal wave is seen in the brown, gold, gray, and black prints on every page and is heard in the urgency with which the story is told.

Rain Makes Applesauce. Julian Scheer. Illustrated by Marvin Bileck. Holiday.
Each two-page spread contains a nonsense line that always ends with "And rain makes applesauce" and the accusation, "Oh you're just talking silly talk." Illustrations in rich but delicate colors have an almost surrealistic effect and add a sophisticated tone.

1964 Award

Where the Wild Things Are
Maurice Sendak   Harper

Sent to bed without any supper, Max travels far to where the wild things are. Taming them with a special magic trick, Max suddenly longs to be at home. The pictures are full of movement and magic, and in several two-page spreads without text they are absolutely boisterous.

HONORS

Swimmy. Leo Lionni. Pantheon.
Swimmy, a small, black fish, convinces a school of small fish to swim in the formation of a large fish, thus proving that in numbers there is strength. The watery world is filled with shapes, patterns, and colors.

All in the Morning Early. Sorche Nic Leodhas, pseud. (Leclaire Alger). Illustrated by Evaline Ness. Holt.
Asked by his mother to take a sack of corn to the mill, Sandy starts on his way. With each animal or person he meets along the way, the cumulative rhythmic tale grows longer. The drawings, with their overlapping colors, place the scene in Scotland, where the old rhyme originated.

Mother Goose and Nursery Rhymes. Illustrated by Philip Reed. Atheneum.
Wood engravings, both serious and silly in approach, decorate nearly all sixty-six rhymes and proverbs included in this collection. Large print, generous margins, crisp and colorful engravings, and just one or two nursery rhymes a page encourage a lingering look at each illustration.

1963 Award

The Snowy Day
Ezra Jack Keats   Viking

Peter has fun on a snow-covered day making tracks and angels in the snow, building a snowman, and even trying to save a snowball for later. Spare, colorful collage pictures capture the wonder of a small child's trudge through new snow.

HONORS

The Sun Is a Golden Earring. Natalia M. Belting. Illustrated by
Bernarda Bryson. Holt.

People have always wondered about nature and have made up stories and
sayings to explain natural phenomena. The author's collection of ancient
sayings from folklore is reproduced here. The drawings lend an effective
ethereal spirit to the book.

Mr. Rabbit and the Lovely Present. Charlotte Zolotow. Illustrated by
Maurice Sendak. Harper.

A little girl seeks birthday present advice from the wonderfully lanky,
long-legged Mr. Rabbit. As the two wander through beautiful pastel scenes,
she explains that her mother likes colors. They discuss many objects that are
of the colors her mother likes the best.

1962 Award

Once a Mouse
Retold and illustrated by Marcia Brown   Scribner

The brief, carefully chosen text taken from a fable of ancient India tells of a
hermit magician that changes a mouse into a cat, a dog, a tiger, and finally
back into a mouse again. Illustrated in woodcuts filled with patterns, the
overlaying of the gold, red, and black add even more dimension.

HONORS

The Day We Saw the Sun Come Up. Alice E. Goudey. Illustrated by
Adrienne Adams. Scribner.

In this poetic science book, two children get up very early in the morning and
see the sun come up. They watch their long shadows and see what happens to
them later in the day. Illustrations are in appropriate colors—gray and shad-
owy in the early morning, bright and clear at noon.

Little Bear's Visit. Else H. Minarik. Illustrated by Maurice Sendak.
Harper.

Little Bear thoroughly enjoys his visit with his grandparents and delights in
the stories they tell. The brown, green, and black-and-white illustrations of
the cuddly, loving Little Bear and his fully clothed grandparents are enhanced with fine crosshatching.

The Fox Went Out on a Chilly Night: An Old Song. Illustrated by Peter Spier.
Doubleday.

Alternating double-page spreads of full-color and black-and-white detailed
drawings greatly extend the story told in the old song. The fox kills a duck
and a goose, outruns the farmer, and dines with his wife with fork and knife
while the ten little pups chew on the "bones-o." The musical score is ap-
pended.

1961 Award

Baboushka and the Three Kings — Ruth Robbins
Illustrated by Nicolas Sidjakov — Parnassus

Old Baboushka declined to go with the three kings in search of the Child. Now, every year at Christmastime she continues her endless, endless search. On her way she leaves gifts for children. Rich, four-color, angular pictures in primitive style adorn the Russian tale.

HONOR

Inch by Inch. Leo Lionni. Obolensky.

An inchworm saves himself from being eaten because he is able to measure things—a robin's tail, a flamingo's neck, a humming bird's body. But when asked to measure the nightingale's song, the inchworm must think fast. The bright green inchworm inches its way out of sight through a collage of grass.

1960 Award

Nine Days to Christmas
Marie Hall Ets and Aurora Labastida
Illustrated by Marie Hall Ets — Viking

Now that she is in kindergarten, Ceci is old enough to join in the *posadas*—part of the special Christmas celebration that begins nine days before Christmas. Anticipation mounts as Ceci chooses her own piñata. Soft, gray backgrounds with splashes of bright colors project the warmth and excitement of the Mexican tradition in an urban setting.

HONORS

Houses from the Sea. Alice E. Goudey. Illustrated by Adrienne Adams. Scribner.

Soft watercolor washes combine with poetic text to set the tone of this quiet, informative story. Two children gather shells along the coast and talk about the various shapes of the shells. An introduction and afterword provide more scientific information.

The Moon Jumpers. Janice May Udry. Illustrated by Maurice Sendak. Harper.

When the sun goes down, the moon comes up. Four children calling themselves the moon jumpers joyfully play and dance under the moonlit sky before bedtime. Soft night colors add a mystic touch to the simple story.

1959 Award

Chanticleer and the Fox
Adapted from Chaucer's Canterbury Tales
Illustrated by Barbara Cooney   Crowell

The old fable of the proud rooster and the wily fox was retold by Chaucer in his *Canterbury Tales*. Cooney has adapted that version for children. The text is filled with descriptive language, while the illustrations, rich in color and strong lines, capture medieval times.

HONORS

The House That Jack Built: La Maison Que Jacques A Batie.
Antonio Frasconi.   Harcourt.

> An old cumulative nursery rhyme, told in English and French, is illustrated with brilliantly colored woodcuts. A review at the end of the text asks questions in English and provides answers in French.

What Do You Say, Dear?   Sesyle Joslin.   Illustrated by Maurice Sendak.
W. R. Scott.

> Absurdly funny and outlandish situations are presented, followed by the question, "what do you say, dear?" and the proper rule of etiquette. Blue, yellow, and black illustrations continue the hilarity, even though the rule is presented straightforwardly.

Umbrella.   Taro Yashima.   Viking.

> Thrilled with the umbrella and red boots she receives on her third birthday, Momo impatiently waits out the days until it rains. How proud she is when she can finally use her new rain gear! The impressionistic illustrations are filled with brush strokes of red, blues, and yellows and reflect the Japanese culture.

1958 Award

Time of Wonder
Robert McCloskey   Viking

McCloskey celebrates in prose and painting the island where he lives. The alternately quiet and boisterous moods of nature are peacefully or dramatically recounted. The children of the island explore and enjoy the changing moods as the intensity of the blue and green watercolors shifts with the changes in the weather.

HONORS

Fly High, Fly Low.   Don Freeman.   Viking.

> In a story of love, loyalty, and suspense, the pigeon Sid faces perils while searching for the missing Midge, their nest, and the big letter *B* where their nest is housed. Colorful illustrations reveal scenes of San Francisco.

Anatole and the Cat. Eve Titus. Illustrated by Paul Galdone. McGraw-Hill.

Mouse Anatole, a loving husband and caring father, bicycles through the streets of Paris each night on his way to work. When a cat arrives on the scene, Anatole succeeds where thousands of other mice have failed. Gray drawings with accents of red, white, and blue and a smattering of French words reinforce the setting of the story.

1957 Award

A Tree Is Nice Janice Udry
Illustrated by Marc Simont Harper

Trees are wonderful: They give shade, are fun to climb, are great to swing from, and even give cats a place to hide from dogs. Illustrated with watercolors, this book is a celebration of trees.

HONORS

Gillespie and the Guards. Benjamin Elkin. Illustrated by James Daugherty. Viking.

Gillespie sets out to fool the three haughty guards by the old trick of the obvious. Robust illustrations are filled with humor and point with pride to the little boy who outsmarts the smug guards.

Lion. William Pène du Bois. Viking.

High in the sky, in the place where animals are invented, the boss comes up with a wonderful new name for an animal—"lion." His difficulty in deciding what it should look like is depicted in a line drawing of his original idea of a lion, complete with feathers, fur, and fish scales.

Mr. Penny's Race Horse. Marie Hall Ets. Viking.

Mr. Penny promises his animals a ride on the Ferris wheel if they win enough prize money at the fair. In an attempt to make sure they win first prize, the animals cause chaos. The dark black-and-white illustrations of the farm and the fair are all set within a border.

Anatole. Eve Titus. Illustrated by Paul Galdone. McGraw-Hill.

Shocked and shaken when he overhears humans saying that mice are terrible and dirty, Anatole the mouse determines to give humans something in return for the food he takes. Red, white, blue, and gray illustrations alternate with black-and-white ones as they reveal the world from the perspective of a French mouse.

1 Is One. Tasha Tudor. Walck.

Simple verse and delicate old-fashioned paintings and drawings introduce numerals from one to twenty. Each page is bordered with charming drawings of wild flowers. Within the borders children and scenes from nature represent the number depicted.

1956 Award

Frog Went A-Courtin'
Retold by John Langstaff
Illustrated by Feodor Rojankovsky   Harcourt

In this story based on an old song and written in snappy, rhyming couplets, a frog courts Miss Mousie, and soon the insects and small animals scurry about preparing for the wedding feast. Full-color illustrations alternate with black-and-white and frog green ones, climaxing in a state of confusion as the cat joins the feast. Music is included.

HONORS

Play with Me.   Marie Hall Ets.   Viking.

Reaching out to touch the woodland animals that she wants to play with, the little girl finds that they all run from her. She sits very still, and one by one the animals come close to her. Repetition in the story is loosely carried out in the quiet drawings as the girl never strays far from the pond.

Crow Boy.   Taro Yashima.   Viking.

In a deeply sensitive school story, Chibi, a very shy boy, is taunted by his classmates for years. A new teacher takes the time to talk to Chibi and discovers his talents. Set in a Japanese village, the story is illustrated with brush strokes that reflect an economy of style.

1955 Award

Cinderella, or the Little Glass Slipper
Illustrated and translated from Charles Perrault
by Marcia Brown   Scribner

Freely translated from Charles Perrault's French tale, this story of Cinderella, her ugly stepsisters, the fairy godmother, and the glass slipper is enhanced with illustrations that fairly dance across the pages with pink and aqua colors and whispy black lines. The enchanting pictures capture the romance of the tale.

HONORS

Wheel on the Chimney.   Margaret Wise Brown.   Illustrated by Tibor Gergely. Lippincott.

Storks come from Africa to build their nest on the chimney and live by the cool, green rivers of Hungary. When fall comes they fly south over towns, rivers, and bridges. The full-page paintings of the Mediterranean city, the pink flamingos, and the flock of white storks in flight are striking in color.

The Thanksgiving Story.   Alice Dalgliesh.   Illustrated by Helen Sewell.
   Scribner.
   Events leading up to the first Thanksgiving celebration in Plymouth Colony
   are told with the Hopkins family as the focus. Flat, primitive color illustrations of people are interspersed with rust-colored silhouettes of objects important to the Pilgrims in their new land.

Book of Nursery and Mother Goose Rhymes.   Illustrated by
   Marguerite de Angeli.   Doubleday.
   Three hundred seventy-six rhymes are delicately illustrated in this oversized
   book. A soft, cheerful tone pervades the sketches, many of which were inspired by scenes of the English countryside. A small sketch of a goose appears on almost every page.

1954 Award

Madeline's Rescue
Ludwig Bemelmans   Viking

When Madeline is rescued from the river by a dog, the dog becomes the heroine of the convent school. The girls love the dog, but the trustees say it
must go. Bright, irrepressible pictures match the indomitable spirit of the
little French girl.

HONORS

The Steadfast Tin Soldier.   Hans Christian Andersen, translated by
   M. R. James.   Illustrated by Marcia Brown.   Scribner.
   Five-and-twenty tin soldiers, all made from the same tin spoon, look alike except for the last one made. He stands firmly on his one leg. It is he who falls in
   love with the toy ballerina. Their tragic story is enhanced with blue-violet
   and red drawings.

Green Eyes.   A. Birnbaum.   Capitol.
   An all-white cat with long whiskers and green eyes is about to celebrate his
   first birthday. In simple text and drawings reminiscent of the bold lines of
   children's art, the tale of Green Eyes's activities in the four seasons that have
   just passed unfolds.

A Very Special House.   Ruth Krauss.   Illustrated by Maurice Sendak.
   Harper.
   The little boy is blissfully happy as he tells of a house he knows where he puts
   his feet on the table, bounces on the bed, and swings on the door. It is a place
   where everyone yells for more, and no one ever says "stop." Line illustrations seem to frolic across the page, and only at the end is it revealed that the
   story is a triumph of imaginary play.

Journey Cake, Ho!   Ruth Sawyer.   Illustrated by Robert McCloskey.   Viking.
   When there is only enough food left to feed two, not three, the bound-out boy

is sent on his way with a huge Journey Cake. The cake breaks free, bounces down the road, and soon animal after animal joins the chase until they all end up where the boy started. Expressive illustrations provide the feel of an American folktale.

When Will the World Be Mine? Miriam Schlein. Illustrated by Jean Charlot. W. R. Scott.

Little Snowshoe Rabbit is born in the spring. His mother spends much of the year protecting and teaching him. She gently shows him how to adapt to the world around him, and in that way the world becomes his. The lithographs in browns and greens show stylized rabbits and their view of the world.

1953 Award

The Biggest Bear
Lynd Ward   Houghton

Humiliated because his family has the only barn that never has a bear skin hanging on it, Johnny sets out with his shotgun in search of a bear. He returns home with a live, cuddly, hungry bear cub that soon grows into a big, rambunctious, voracious bear. The illustrations are sensitive, strong, and robust.

HONORS

Ape in a Cape: An Alphabet of Odd Animals. Fritz Eichenberg. Harcourt.

Bold, humorous, colorful pictures and short, nonsense verses combine to create a lively alphabet book. From the "bear in despair" to the "yak with a pack," there is wonderful fun and imagination on each page.

Five Little Monkeys. Juliet Kepes. Houghton.

Buzzo, Binki, Bulu, Bibi, and Bali are the little mischievous monkeys who, because of their irritating tricks, cause the other jungle animals to band together to punish them. Alternating pages of color and black-and-white illustrations show the stylized monkeys acting up.

One Morning in Maine. Robert McCloskey. Viking.

While clam digging with her father, Sally loses a tooth that falls amongst the pebbles of the beach. Large, dark blue lithographs depict the great pride associated with losing the first baby tooth. All the characters in the small Maine town enjoy Sally's joy.

Puss in Boots. Illustrated and translated from Charles Perrault by Marcia Brown. Scribner.

The youngest son inherits a cat and realizes that after eating it he will have nothing left. Crafty Puss in Boots tells his master to do as he says and all will be well, and indeed it is! Puss, with his fine red boots, is shown as a grand, swashbuckling character who takes command of all the folderol of a French court.

The Storm Book. Charlotte Zolotow. Illustrated by Margaret Bloy Graham. Harper.

A little boy watches in wonder as the day turns ominously gray and still, a storm approaches, and breaks forth. He asks his mother questions and she replies with reassuring answers. Each two-page spread of text is followed by a double-page spread of illustrations, most of them showing a driving rain.

1952 Award

Finders Keepers

Will, pseud. (William Lipkind)   Illustrated by Nicolas,
pseud. (Nicolas Mordvinoff)   Harcourt

Two dogs find a bone. One saw it first; the other touched it first. Unable to decide who owns it, they bury it and go off to seek the opinion of others and in so doing almost lose the bone to another dog. The bold use of color adds spark and flair to the simple story.

HONORS

Skipper John's Cook. Marcia Brown. Scribner.

Beans! That was the trouble. The Skipper's crew refuses to sign on until a cook is found who does not fix beans morning, noon, and night. Young Si is hired on. After he has fried his 259th fish, the crew wants to know what else he can cook. Beans! Illustrations capture the expressions of the crew—and of the pots and pans.

Bear Party. William Pène du Bois. Viking.

When the koala bears become very angry with each other, it is "the wise old bear who lives at the top of the tallest Eucalyptus tree" who decides what to do. The koala bears are shown dressed in all the finery of a masked costume party, while wonderful onomatopoeic words describe the sounds of the musical instruments.

Mr. T. W. Anthony Woo. Marie Hall Ets. Viking.

Pandemonium reigns at the cobbler's when his dog and cat fight each other, and then both chase Mr. T. W. Anthony Woo, the mouse. Sister and her parrot move in, and things go from bad to worse until the enemies band together to create peace. Illustrations are contained within borders and suggest the control the cobbler wishes he had.

Feather Mountain. Elizabeth Olds. Houghton.

At one time all birds were naked and pink and featherless. One day they ask the Great Spirit to give them coverings. Black-and-white and color pictures depict the birds as they scurry around finding just the right colors to blend with their habitats.

All Falling Down. Gene Zion. Illustrated by Margaret Bloy Graham. Harper.

So many things fall—petals, rain, apples, even Daddy's book when his head begins to nod. This quiet, reflective book is illustrated with pastel colors. There is a surprise ending when Daddy tosses the baby in the air.

1951 Award

The Egg Tree
Katherine Milhous   Scribner

An Easter morning egg hunt leads to the discovery of long forgotten decorated eggs. With them the family begins a new tradition. Pennsylvania Dutch folk designs border many of the pages; the colors found in hex signs dominate the paintings that interpret the story.

HONORS

Dick Whittington and His Cat. Marcia Brown. Scribner.

Artistic linoleum block cuts have humor and charm. They illustrate a simple retelling of the folktale of the boy who was made wealthy because he listened to his cat.

If I Ran the Zoo. Dr. Seuss, pseud. (Theodor Seuss Geisel). Random House.

Young Gerald McGrew likes the zoo but knows that if he ran it he would make some changes. He imagines all kinds of fantastic beasts with wonderfully creative names and unusual shapes and habits. Zany, whimsical illustrations are perfect for the imaginative verse.

The Two Reds. Will, pseud. (William Lipkind). Illustrated by Nicolas, pseud. (Nicolas Mordvinoff). Harcourt.

Red, the boy, sets out to play at the same time Red, an independent cat, sets out for food. The sense of impending chaos mounts as each gets in trouble at the same time in different parts of town. Sparse line drawings with brilliant splashes of red add spark to the illustrations.

T-Bone, the Baby Sitter. Clare Turlay Newberry. Harper.

T-Bone the cat loves to sit. That is what makes him such a fine baby-sitter—until the day he awakens with a twinkle in his eye, full of mischief. Expressive illustrations show the baby's extreme displeasure when T-Bone is taken away to the country and his pleasure when he returns.

The Most Wonderful Doll in the World. Phyllis McGinley. Illustrated by Helen Stone. Lippincott.

Duley loses a new doll. Her imagination runs wild as she describes the lost and most wonderful doll in the world as she wants it to be, not as it is. The book is decorated with four-color and black-and-white illustrations and borders.

1950 Award

Song of the Swallows
Leo Politi   Scribner

The bell ringer and gardener of the mission church in Capistrano tells Juan the history of the mission churches and of the return of the swallows every St. Joseph's Day. Pinks, grays, yellows, and greens in muted tones convey friendship and a respect for nature. Two songs are included in the text.

HONORS

Henry Fisherman. Marcia Brown. Scribner.

To be a fisherman a boy has to be able to swim very fast in case a shark is near. As the day when Juan will be allowed on the fishing boat draws closer, sights and sounds of a childhood in the Virgin Islands are portrayed in brown, coral, yellow, and green.

The Wild Birthday Cake. Lavinia R. Davis. Illustrated by Hildegard Woodward. Doubleday.

Johnny is so excited about going on an adventurous hike that he almost forgets his friend's seventy-fifth birthday. On his hike he catches a wild duck and later gives it to his friend as a gift. Abundant on the pages are the yellows and greens of spring.

Bartholomew and the Oobleck. Dr. Seuss, pseud. (Theodor Seuss Geisel). Random House.

Tired of snow, fog, rain, and sunshine, the king wants something new to fall from the sky. What he gets are green, gooey globs of oobleck that threaten to destroy the kingdom. Comical illustrations in black-and-white become greener and greener as the oobleck spreads.

America's Ethan Allen. Stewart Holbrook. Illustrated by Lynd Ward. Houghton.

Brave and rebellious Ethan Allen is born in the wilds of the old colony of Connecticut. He grows into a rugged frontier hero who leads the Green Mountain Boys. The illustrations and writing style resound with patriotism and historical significance.

The Happy Day. Ruth Krauss. Illustrated by Marc Simont. Harper.

The woodland animals are all in their winter's sleep when something causes them to open their eyes and sniff. Suspense mounts as they all race toward the thing that has caused them to awaken. Black-and-white drawings portray joyous animals as they leap around a bright yellow flower—the first sign of spring and the only color in the book.

1949 Award

The Big Snow
Berta and Elmer Hader   Macmillan

When they see the wild geese flying overhead, all the woodland animals scurry to get ready for winter. After the big snow they slowly emerge to find food. Black-and-white drawings are occasionally interspersed with full-color paintings.

HONORS

Blueberries for Sal. Robert McCloskey. Viking.

On the same day that Little Sal and her mother go to Blueberry Hill to pick blueberries, so do Little Bear and his mother. Soon a mix-up in mothers occurs. Dark blue-and-white type and drawings promote gentle humor against the ruggedness of Blueberry Hill.

All Around the Town. Phyllis McGinley.   Illustrated by Helen Stone. Lippincott.

Snappy rhythm of the text and splashes of color in the illustrations capture the gaiety and pace of city life. Each verse is about a city sight and the rhymes are arranged in alphabetical order, from Aeroplane to Zoo.

Juanita. Leo Politi. Scribner.

As Easter draws near, Juanita and her friends join in the parade for the Blessing of the Animals at the Old Mission Church. The text is lovingly illustrated and interspersed with some songs, making the warmth of a close-knit community in old Los Angeles come alive.

Fish in the Air. Kurt Wiese. Viking.

On their way to fly a great big kite, Fish and his kite are grabbed by a Tai Fung, or big wind. It sends them on a high-flying adventure. Colorful paintings portray the excitement caused when Fish flies over town and countryside.

1948 Award

White Snow, Bright Snow
Alvin Tresselt   Illustrated by Roger Duvoisin   Lothrop

Slowly the snow begins to fall and the adults busy themselves preparing for it. The children revel in it. A dark blue background gives way to white as the heavy snow melts and spring breaks forth. Reds and yellows provide a cheerful balance.

HONORS

Stone Soup. Marcia Brown. Scribner.
An inhospitable town refuses to help three hungry soldiers. When the soldiers decide to make a soup of stones, curiosity overcomes the peasants and they learn a lesson in cooperation. Orange and brown pictures portray peasant life in a long-ago French village.

Roger and the Fox. Lavinia R. Davis. Illustrated by Hildegard Woodward. Doubleday.
Roger wants to see the wild fox and tries many times before he figures out how to be quick and quiet enough to do it. The pictures turn from the warm hues of fall to the cold blues of winter before patience and ingenuity finally pay off.

McElligot's Pool. Dr. Seuss, pseud. (Theodor Seuss Geisel). Random House.
Told that he is some sort of fool for trying to catch fish in McElligot's pool, Marco visualizes the possibility that the pool is connected to the sea. Wonderfully imaginative creatures with fantastic names swim across the pages of this story told in verse.

Song of Robin Hood. Edited by Anne Malcolmson. Designed and illustrated by Virginia Lee Burton. Houghton.
Eighteen ballads of Robin Hood, most traced back to their original tunes, are exuberantly presented in verse, music, and art. The five hundred verses are decorated in a style reminiscent of miniature drawings of the fifteenth century. Its words meant to be sung not read, the book provides an energetic and lyrical introduction to the famous Robin Hood.

Bambino the Clown. Georges Schreiber. Viking.
The full colors and excitement of a circus clown's act are experienced by a sad young boy whom Bambino befriends. Peter is invited into the clown's dressing room, watches him apply his makeup, and becomes a very funny part of the show.

1947 Award

The Little Island
Golden MacDonald, pseud. (Margaret Wise Brown)
Illustrated by Leonard Weisgard Doubleday
The seasons come and go and little by little the small island changes. One day a kitten visits the island and discovers that it does not stand alone but is connected underwater to land. The moods of the mostly green and blue drawings change with the seasons.

HONORS

Boats on the River. Marjorie Flack.   Illustrated by Jay Hyde Barnum.   Viking.

There are warships, ocean liners, rowboats, and many other boats on the river that flows by the city and out to sea. Full-color paintings show close and distant views of the boats.

Timothy Turtle.   Al Graham.   Illustrated by Tony Palazzo.   Welch.

On the day Timothy flips over on his back, each animal tries to help him right himself. The wise frog tells the other animals that what they could not do as individuals they can do as a group. Action-packed drawings add tautness and humor to the tale.

Pedro, the Angel of Olvera Street.   Leo Politi.   Scribner.

Young Pedro, who sings like an angel, leads *La Posada,* the Christmas procession, on Olvera Street in Los Angeles. For nine consecutive nights he wears red wings and sings carols of Christian pilgrims. The soft colors reflect the solemnity of the procession. Music is included.

Rain Drop Splash.   Alvin Tresselt.   Illustrated by Leonard Weisgard.   Lothrop.

A single rain drop splashes down. Soon it is joined by others, and a puddle is formed. The puddle grows bigger and bigger until the rain drops at last become the sea, and the rain stops. The poetic patterns of the text and the drenched look of the pictures provide a closeness to nature.

Sing in Praise: A Collection of the Best Loved Hymns.   Opal Wheeler. Illustrated by Marjorie Torrey.   Dutton.

Twenty-five perennially popular Christian hymns have been arranged to simple piano scores. Most of the hymns are accompanied by a laudatory story about how the particular words or melody came to be written. Romanticized illustrations show pious children looking heavenward.

1946 Award

The Rooster Crows
Maud and Miska Petersham   Macmillan

A potpourri of the rhymes, jingles, and chants of American children is treated to a variety of visual interpretations. Each rhyme is illustrated with humor and rhythm.

HONORS

Little Lost Lamb.   Golden MacDonald, pseud. (Margaret Wise Brown). Illustrated by Leonard Weisgard.   Doubleday.

When the little black lamb strays from the rest of the flock, the little shepherd and his sheepdog go into the perilous night in search of it. The mood of the story changes from bright, frolicsome pictures of the frisky lamb to dark browns that reflect the concern the boy has for the lost animal.

My Mother Is the Most Beautiful Woman in the World. Becky Reyher. Illustrated by Ruth Gannett. Lothrop.

When a little girl becomes lost, she describes her mother with her heart not with her eyes. Colorful pictures reflect the spirit of the old Russian proverb, "We do not love people because they are beautiful, but they seem beautiful to us because we love them."

Sing Mother Goose. Music by Opal Wheeler. Illustrated by Marjorie Torrey. Dutton.

Fifty-two of the most familiar Mother Goose nursery rhymes have been arranged to original, sprightly music. The piano scores and the rhymes are accompanied by illustrations of children, many of whom are in late-Victorian dress.

You Can Write Chinese. Kurt Wiese. Viking.

In China in the 1940s, a classroom of boys receives a language lesson. The teacher explains that there are no letters in the Chinese language, only words based on ancient pictures. Most of the book consists of large drawings of Chinese characters superimposed on drawings of objects that represent the words.

────────────────── **1945 Award** ──────────────────

Prayer for a Child   Rachel Field
Illustrated by Elizabeth Orton Jones   Macmillan

A child's bedtime prayer asks for blessings on things that are familiar to small children with such lines as, "Bless other children, far and near, And keep them safe and free from fear." Brief lines of the prayer are illustrated with full-page, reverent golden-toned drawings.

HONORS

In the Forest. Marie Hall Ets. Viking.

With his new horn and paper hat a little boy takes a walk in the forest, and along the way he meets storks, kangaroos, bears, and other animals who join his parade. All disappear when the boy's father comes hunting for him. There is a strong contrast between the white figures and the black forest backgrounds.

Yonie Wondernose. Marguerite de Angeli. Doubleday.

His father has promised him something very special as soon as seven-year-old Yonie learns to handle responsibilities like a man. Strongly depicted in the illustrations and the text is the hard but cheerful way of life on an Amish farm.

The Christmas Anna Angel. Ruth Sawyer. Illustrated by Kate Seredy. Viking.

In a story set in Hungary during the war, Anna longs for a Christmas cake shaped like a little clock. The deprivations caused by the war contrast with the happy family traditions of Christmas. While heavy on text, the book has several illustrations reflective of the folk culture.

Mother Goose.   Illustrated by Tasha Tudor.   Oxford University Press.
Seventy-seven Mother Goose rhymes are gathered together in this small book. Many of the rhymes are familiar, but some are those usually found only in complete works. Quaint, soft-colored pictures abound on every page.

1944 Award

Many Moons   James Thurber
Illustrated by Louis Slobodkin   Harcourt

After eating too many raspberry tarts, the princess declares that if she can have the moon she will be well again. The wisdom of the royal advisors fails. The common sense of the jester prevails. Washes of pinks and blues complement the whimsy of the humorous fantasy.

HONORS

A Child's Good Night Book.   Margaret Wise Brown.   Illustrated by Jean Charlot.   W. R. Scott.
Night has come and everything is going to sleep. Animals, children, and even engines are sleepy. The brief story ends with a prayer to bless and guard "small things that have no words." The repetitious phrases and drawings are designed to bring on drowsiness.

Good-Luck Horse.   Chih-Yi Chan.   Illustrated by Plato Chan.   Whittlesey.
A lonely boy in ancient China creates a very small paper horse that he can hold in his hand. Magically the horse becomes real. Although the magician names it "Good-Luck Horse," the story proves that sometimes good luck is bad luck and vice versa. The adventures of the horse are re-created in the line and wash drawings.

The Mighty Hunter.   Berta and Elmer Hader.   Macmillan.
Little Brave Heart's mother tells him to go to school so he can grow up to be a wise leader, but he goes hunting instead. Each animal in turn tells him that there is a better animal to shoot. The bear chastises him for hunting for "fun," and chases him to school. The illustrations alternate between black-and-white and desert colors.

Small Rain: Verses from the Bible.   Verses selected by Jessie Orton Jones.
Illustrated by Elizabeth Orton Jones.   Viking.
Brief Bible verses taken from the King James Version of the Old and New Testaments are illustrated with children doing everyday things—romping, playing, sitting quietly, sharing, running, crying, and sleeping. Each verse relates in some way to what the children are doing.

Pierre Pigeon.   Lee Kingman.   Illustrated by Arnold E. Bare.   Houghton.

Seven-year-old Pierre has long been fascinated by the boat-in-bottle in the shop. Finally he purchases it, and before he gets it home he breaks it. Studying the broken model, he succeeds in figuring out how the boat got into the bottle. Gray, green, and peach tones reflect a Canadian fishing village.

1943 Award

The Little House
Virginia Lee Burton   Houghton

Built long ago far out in the country, the Little House is now surrounded by the city. Circular shapes abound in the illustrations and the lines of type. Bright, happy colors give way to dark, moody ones as progress overtakes the house. Light colors return when the house is moved to a new countryside.

HONORS

Dash and Dart.   Mary and Conrad Buff.   Viking.

In simple, poetic text and mood-capturing sepia paintings, the first year in the life of two fawns is described. A great reverence for nature is felt throughout the book.

Marshmallow.   Clare Turlay Newberry.   Harper.

Oliver the cat lives a blissful life of eating and sleeping until the lady who takes care of him brings home a bundle of live, soft fur. Suddenly Oliver is terrified when he is confronted with a bunny named Marshmallow. The pictures show how their relationship grows until they both curl up together.

1942 Award

Make Way for Ducklings
Robert McCloskey   Viking

Having hatched her ducklings and taught them to march nicely in single file, Mrs. Mallard decides to take them straight through Boston's busy streets to their new home in the Public Garden and pond. Sketchy brown drawings humorously show the ordeal the mallards face.

HONORS

In My Mother's House.   Ann Nolan Clark.   Illustrated by Velino Herrera. Viking.

Daily life of the pueblo as seen through the eyes of the children is described in a rhythmic, simple prose. Many aspects of life—houses, food, clothing, and agriculture—are pictured. Tribal designs and pen-and-ink and color drawings depict the Tawa life.

Nothing at All. Wanda Gág. Coward.

Three orphan dogs, two visible and one invisible, are adopted by two children. It takes a jackdaw, some magic, and a lot of energetic work by Nothing At All to become Something After All. Intriguing, lightly colored lithographs show the invisible become visible.

Paddle-to-the-Sea. Holling C. Holling. Houghton.

In the Canadian wilderness, a young boy carves a canoe with an Indian figure seated in it, then launches it from Lake Nipigon. The text and illustrations are filled with information about the scenes the canoe passes, from the quiet byways, to a sawmill, to a raging forest fire.

An American ABC. Maud and Miska Petersham. Macmillan.

Familiar symbols, historic places, and legendary figures form the basis of this patriotic interpretation of the alphabet. Decorated in red, white, blue, and black, each letter provides a brief lesson in American history. The strength and courage of those who shaped America are visible in the drawings.

1941 Award

They Were Strong and Good Robert Lawson Viking

Writing of his mother and father and their mothers and fathers, Lawson says they, like the ancestors of many others, were never famous but were "strong and good" and helped to build America. Line-and-brush drawings are sometimes humorous but more often depict the strength and goodness of the land and its people.

HONOR

April's Kittens. Clare Turlay Newberry. Harper.

After her cat has kittens, April must decide on the one cat to keep. Illustrations of the black cats make them look fuzzy and furry. Occasional touches of red add a dash of color.

1940 Award

Abraham Lincoln
Ingri and Edgar Parin d'Aulaire Doubleday

Well-known anecdotes of Lincoln, particularly of his youth and prairie years, are recounted with strength and humor in this picture biography. Lithographs in color and black and white reveal details of American life in the 1800s.

HONORS

Madeline. Ludwig Bemelmans. Viking.

High-spirited Madeline may be the smallest of the twelve little girls at Miss Clavel's school, but she is by far the bravest. Lilting rhythmic text and simple, childlike paintings provide a tour of Paris and introduce a spunky heroine.

The Ageless Story. Illustrated by Lauren Ford. Dodd.

The story of the Christ Child is told through Gregorian music, biblical text, and illustrations that are an adaptation of illuminated manuscripts. The illustrations are a blend of early Renaissance religious art in a New England setting.

Cock-a-Doodle-Doo. Berta and Elmer Hader. Macmillan.

In a reversal of the story of the Ugly Duckling, a chick is hatched by a duck. The ducklings make fun of him, and soon the chick goes off in search of others like him. In alternating color and black-and-white pictures he faces several perils before landing in the hen house.

1939 Award

Mei Li
Thomas Handforth   Doubleday

The New Year Fair is in the city, and Mei Li's brother has been told that he can go, but little girls have to stay home. Strong, bold line drawings present many aspects of Chinese culture and customs as they follow the irrepressible Mei Li, who sneaks off for a grand time at the fair.

HONORS

The Forest Pool. Laura Adams Armer. Longmans.

Glowing with the bright golden colors of South America, stylized pictures show two boys as they go in search of the iguana in the bell-flower tree. The boys ponder the animals that know so much but never reveal their secrets.

Andy and the Lion. James Daugherty. Viking.

The old story of Androcles and the lion is retold in a modern setting. Andy signs out a book about lions from the library. The next day he comes upon a lion with a thorn stuck in his paw. Told and illustrated with robust tall-tale humor, the twists of the tale lead to a fine friendship.

Snow White and the Seven Dwarfs. Translated and illustrated by Wanda Gág. Coward.

In this little book the Brothers Grimm story of the vain, wicked stepmother, the seven dwarfs, and the beautiful princess is retold with much repetition. The black-and-white drawings are filled with rounded shapes that continue the repetitiousness of the story.

Wee Gillis. Munro Leaf. Illustrated by Robert Lawson. Viking.
The Highland relatives want Wee Gillis to stalk stags with them. The Lowland relatives want him to tend the cows. After years of doing both, Wee Gillis has powerful lungs from calling the cows, and he has learned to sit very still from stalking stags—just the skills needed to play a bagpipe! Line drawings sparkle with humorous spirit.

Barkis. Clare Turlay Newberry. Harper.
A bickering brother and sister squabble over the ownership of a new puppy and cat. They finally reach a solution that makes them both happy. Soft brown-and-black drawings of the winsome cat and dog are set against white backgrounds.

1938 Award

Animals of the Bible, a Picture Book
Text selected by Helen Dean Fish
Illustrated by Dorothy P. Lathrop   Lippincott

The Old and New Testaments of the King James Version are the sources for thirty-one stories about animals. Black-and-white full-page illustrations include the flora of biblical lands and portray the animals with reverence.

HONORS

Seven Simeons: A Russian Tale. Retold and illustrated by Boris Artzybasheff. Viking.
King Douda, wise, rich, strong, and very handsome, decides to marry a princess as beautiful as himself. To help him in his quest, he engages seven brothers, each of whom has a special skill that, by the tale's end, is used in a most unusual manner. Love triumphs in the end in this whimsically decorated book with neat color line drawings.

Four and Twenty Blackbirds. Compiled by Helen Dean Fish. Illustrated by Robert Lawson. Stokes.
The twenty-four nursery rhymes found here were culled from out-of-print books or "rescued from memories of older people." Most are long and filled with the jingling and sturdy humor of traditional nursery rhymes. They are illustrated with vigorous drawings in black and green. Simple music is given for those rhymes that have tunes.

The Media
Used in Caldecott Picture Books:
Notes toward a Definitive List

Christine Behrmann

Since 1938 more than one hundred artists have illustrated picture books that have won a Caldecott Award or been named Caldecott Honor Books. Each of these books has won the accolade because of the quality of its illustrator's distinctive style, a style that has evoked images and ideas in the reader's mind that remain long after the book is closed. As the book is reviewed and discussed, we talk much about the artist's imagination, talent, and unique eye. Mentioned less often is the physical process by which the images imagined by that unique eye come to life and the role of the artist's medium (paint, lithography, pen and ink, etc.) in that process. In the fifty years since the Caldecott Award was first given, there has apparently been no systematic attempt to list the media used to create the honored picture books. This is a loss, because it is scholarly information useful to the study of children's literature, and because it is a humbling and educating experience to see the care, skill, and sheer craftsmanship that go into the creation of a truly distinguished picture book. This article is an initial attempt to fill the void.

What follows must be a work in progress, as digging out this information is a process that involves not only library research, but also correspondence with the artist, editor, or art director, and with other collections. In some cases, the information may be lost forever because it was never written down in bibliographic descriptions, and the author and the publisher are no longer available to be questioned. It is heartening to note that some publishers, such as Dial and Greenwillow, are beginning to list—in the books themselves—the media used in creating the pictures. This practice will certainly aid in the appreciation of the picture book as art.

Reprinted, with changes, from *Journal of Youth Services in Libraries* (Winter 1988): 198–212. Christine Behrmann was Children's Materials Specialist, Office of Children's Services, New York Public Library.

The data listed below are thus, in many cases, preliminary only. Guesses were not made. When hard data were not found, the entry was left blank, except for a question mark. No information was regarded as final unless it was found in two independent secondary sources (review, bibliography, catalog, etc.) or available from one primary source (book, artist, publisher, Caldecott citation). Information from only one secondary source was included but marked preliminary by a question mark in parentheses. Corrections and added information are earnestly solicited. The most important result is to obtain, eventually, a complete, accurate list.

Many deserve thanks for their kind cooperation thus far, but it is most important to single out Lyn Lacey, whose excellent idea this project was.

1938

WINNER *Animals of the Bible* by Helen Dean Fish; Illustrated by Dorothy P. Lathrop (Lippincott)—black-and-white lithographs

HONORS *Seven Simeons* by Boris Artzybasheff (Viking)—pen and ink

Four and Twenty Blackbirds by Helen Dean Fish; Illustrated by Robert Lawson (Stokes)—drawings in pen and tempera

1939

WINNER *Mei Li* by Thomas Handforth (Doubleday)—brush and lithograph pencil (?)

HONORS *The Forest Pool* by Laura Adams Armer (Longmans)—medium not known

Wee Gillis by Munro Leaf; Illustrated by Robert Lawson (Viking)—drawings in pen and tempera

Snow White and the Seven Dwarfs by Wanda Gág (Coward)—lithographs (?)

Barkis by Clare Newberry (Harper)—charcoal pencil and watercolor wash

Andy and the Lion by James Daugherty (Viking)—charcoal rubbed off on light gray transfer and rubbed in (?)

1940

WINNER *Abraham Lincoln* by Ingri and Edgar Parin d'Aulaire (Doubleday)—lithographic pencil on stone

HONORS *Cock-a-Doodle-Doo* by Berta and Elmer Hader (Macmillan)—watercolor

Madeline by Ludwig Bemelmans (Viking)—brush, pen, and watercolor (?)

The Ageless Story; Illustrated by Lauren Ford (Dodd)—painting; touches of gold leaf (?)

1941

WINNER   *They Were Strong and Good* by Robert Lawson (Viking)—brush and ink

HONOR   *April's Kittens* by Clare Newberry (Harper)—ink, charcoal, and watercolor

1942

WINNER   *Make Way for Ducklings* by Robert McCloskey (Viking)—lithographic crayon on stone

HONORS   *An American ABC* by Maud and Miska Petersham (Macmillan)—pencil and preseparated watercolor

In My Mother's House by Ann Nolan Clark; Illustrated by Velino Herrera (Viking)—medium not known

Paddle-to-the-Sea by Holling C. Holling (Houghton)—full-color oil paintings

Nothing at All by Wanda Gág (Coward)—original lithographs in color

1943

WINNER   *The Little House* by Virginia Lee Burton (Houghton)—watercolor

HONORS   *Dash and Dart* by Mary and Conrad Buff (Viking)—lithographs (?)

Marshmallow by Clare Newberry (Harper)—charcoal (?)

1944

WINNER   *Many Moons* by James Thurber; Illustrated by Louis Slobodkin (HBJ)—pen and ink; watercolor

HONORS   *Small Rain:Verses from the Bible;* Selected by Jessie Orton Jones; Illustrated by Elizabeth Orton Jones (Viking)—medium not known

Pierre Pigeon by Lee Kingman; Illustrated by Arnold E. Bare (Houghton)—preseparated gouache and ink drawings

The Mighty Hunter by Berta and Elmer Hader (Macmillan)—watercolor

A Child's Good Night Book by Margaret Wise Brown; Illustrated by Jean Charlot (Scott)—crayon drawings

Good-Luck Horse by Chih–Yi Chan; Illustrated by Plato Chan (Wittlesey)—pen and ink; wash (?)

1945

WINNER   *Prayer for a Child* by Rachel Field; Illustrated by Elizabeth Orton Jones (Macmillan)—pen and ink; watercolor

HONORS   *Mother Goose;* Illustrated by Tasha Tudor (Oxford)—graphite and watercolor (?)

In the Forest by Marie Hall Ets (Viking)—paper batik

Yonie Wondernose by Marguerite de Angeli (Doubleday)—color separations done in pen, ink, pencil, and watercolor

The Christmas Anna Angel by Ruth Sawyer; Illustrated by Kate Seredy (Viking)—medium not known

1946
WINNER   *The Rooster Crows* by Maud and Miska Petersham (Macmillan)—lithograph pencil with color separations on acetate

HONORS   *Little Lost Lamb* by Golden MacDonald; Illustrated by Leonard Weisgard (Doubleday)—medium not known

Sing Mother Goose by Opal Wheeler; Illustrated by Marjorie Torrey (Dutton)—medium not known

My Mother Is the Most Beautiful Woman in the World by Becky Reyher; Illustrated by Ruth C. Gannett (Lothrop)—original gouache and watercolor reproduced by four-match process using lithographic crayon

You Can Write Chinese by Kurt Wiese (Viking)—ink and watercolor separations

1947
WINNER   *The Little Island* By Golden MacDonald; Illustrated by Leonard Weisgard (Doubleday)—gouache

HONORS   *Boats on the River* by Marjorie Flack; Illustrated by Jay Hyde Barnum (Viking)—medium not known

Timothy Turtle by Al Graham; Illustrated by Tony Palazzo (Welch)—black-and-white pen and ink (?)

Pedro, the Angel of Olvera Street by Leo Politi (Scribner)—medium not known

Sing in Praise: A Collection of Best Loved Hymns by Opal Wheeler; Illustrated by Marjorie Torrey (Dutton)—medium not known

Rain Drop Splash by Alvin Tresselt; Illustrated by Leonard Weisgard (Lothrop)—three colors preseparated with india ink on acetate overlays

1948
WINNER   *White Snow, Bright Snow* by Alvin Tresselt; Illustrated by Roger Duvoisin (Lothrop)—acetate separations in india ink

HONORS   *Stone Soup* by Marcia Brown (Scribner)—ink and watercolor (?)

McElligot's Pool by Dr. Seuss (Random)—pencil and watercolor

Bambino the Clown by Georges Schreiber (Viking)—medium not known

Roger and the Fox by Lavinia Davis; Illustrated by Hildegard Woodward (Doubleday)—ink (?)

Song of Robin Hood; Edited by Anne Malcolmson; Illustrated by Virginia Lee Burton (Houghton)—scratchboard

1949
WINNER *The Big Snow* by Berta and Elmer Hader (Macmillan)—watercolor

HONORS *Blueberries for Sal* by Robert McCloskey (Viking)—lithographs (?)

All around the Town by Phyllis McGinley; Illustrated by Helen Stone (Lippincott)—medium not known

Juanita by Leo Politi (Scribner)—tempera (?)

Fish in the Air by Kurt Wiese (Viking)—ink and watercolor

1950
WINNER *Song of the Swallows* by Leo Politi (Scribner)—tempera

HONORS *America's Ethan Allen* by Stewart Holbrook; Illustrated by Lynd Ward (Houghton)—full-color gouache paintings

The Wild Birthday Cake by Lavinia Davis; Illustrated by Hildegard Woodward (Doubleday)—medium not known

The Happy Day by Ruth Krauss; Illustrated by Marc Simont (Harper)—medium not known

Bartholomew and the Oobleck by Dr. Seuss (Random)—pencil, crayon, and watercolor

Henry Fisherman by Marcia Brown (Scribner)—collage (?)

1951
WINNER *The Egg Tree* by Katherine Milhous (Scribner)—tempera

HONORS *Dick Whittington and His Cat* by Marcia Brown (Scribner)—linoleum cuts

The Two Reds by Will Lipkind; Illustrated by Nicolas Mordvinoff (HBJ)—acetate separations using pen, ink, and brush

If I Ran the Zoo by Dr. Seuss (Random)—pencil, ink, and watercolor

The Most Wonderful Doll in the World by Phyllis McGinley; Illustrated by Helen Stone (Lippincott)—medium not known

T-Bone, the Baby Sitter by Clare Newberry (Harper)—pen, ink, and charcoal (?)

1952
WINNER *Finders Keepers* by Will Lipkind; Illustrated by Nicolas Mordvinoff (HBJ)—acetate color separations for line reproduction

HONORS   *Mr. T. W. Anthony Woo* by Marie Hall Ets (Viking)—paper batik

Skipper John's Cook by Marcia Brown (Scribner)—medium not known

All Falling Down by Gene Zion; Illustrated by Margaret Bloy Graham (Harper)—medium not known

Bear Party by William Pène du Bois (Viking)—medium not known

Feather Mountain by Elizabeth Olds (Houghton)—preseparated art and watercolor wash (four-color)

1953
WINNER   *The Biggest Bear* by Lynd Ward (Houghton)—opaque watercolor

HONORS   *Puss in Boots* by Charles Perrault; Illustrated and translated by Marcia Brown (Scribner)—woodcut and watercolor (?)

One Morning in Maine by Robert McCloskey (Viking)—lithographs (?)

Ape in a Cape by Fritz Eichenberg (HBJ)—woodcuts; acetate separations

The Storm Book by Charlotte Zolotow; Illustrated by Margaret Bloy Graham (Harper)—medium not known

Five Little Monkeys by Juliet Kepes (Houghton)—preseparated ink and watercolor wash (four-color)

1954
WINNER   *Madeline's Rescue* by Ludwig Bemelmans (Viking)—brush, pen, and watercolor

HONORS   *Journey Cake, Ho!* by Ruth Sawyer; Illustrated by Robert McCloskey (Viking)—medium not known

When Will the World Be Mine? by Miriam Schlein; Illustrated by Jean Charlot (Scott)—lithographs (?)

The Steadfast Tin Soldier by Hans Christian Andersen; Illustrated by Marcia Brown (Scribner)—medium not known

A Very Special House by Ruth Krauss; Illustrated by Maurice Sendak (Harper)—medium not known

Green Eyes by A. Birnbaum (Capitol)—medium not known

1955
WINNER   *Cinderella* by Charles Perrault; Translated and illustrated by Marcia Brown (Scribner)—gouache, crayon, watercolor, and ink

HONORS   *Book of Nursery and Mother Goose Rhymes;* Illustrated by Marguerite de Angeli (Doubleday)—Sharp Wolf pencils and watercolor

Wheel on the Chimney by Margaret Wise Brown; Illustrated by Tibor Gergely (Lippincott)—gouache (?)

The Thanksgiving Story by Alice Dalgliesh; Illustrated by Helen Sewell (Scribner)—medium not known

1956
WINNER *Frog Went A-Courtin'*; Retold by John Langstaff; Illustrated by Feodor Rojankovsky (HBJ)—brush, ink, and crayon on acetate separations

HONORS *Play with Me* by Marie Hall Ets (Viking)—graphite separations

Crow Boy by Taro Yashima (Viking)—pencil and brush separations

1957
WINNER *A Tree Is Nice* by Janice Udry; Illustrated by Marc Simont (Harper)—gouache over watercolor

HONORS *Mr. Penny's Race Horse* by Marie Hall Ets (Viking)—paper batik

1 Is One by Tasha Tudor (Walck)—graphite and watercolor (?)

Anatole by Eve Titus; Illustrated by Paul Galdone (McGraw)—pen and ink with gray wash over graphite with paper collage (?)

Gillespie and the Guards by Benjamin Elkin; Illustrated by James Daugherty (Viking)—charcoal rubbed off on light gray transfer and inked (?)

Lion by William Pène du Bois (Viking)—pen and india ink; color preseparated on Dinobase with lithographic pencil

1958
WINNER *Time of Wonder* by Robert McCloskey (Viking)—casein

HONORS *Fly High, Fly Low* by Don Freeman (Viking)—colored pencil accented by outlines in ink

Anatole and the Cat by Eve Titus; Illustrated by Paul Galdone (McGraw) —pen and ink with gray wash over graphite with paper collage (?)

1959
WINNER *Chanticleer and the Fox*; Adapted from Chaucer and illustrated by Barbara Cooney (Crowell)—preseparated art: black and white on scratchboard; colors on Dinobase

HONORS *The House That Jack Built* by Antonio Frasconi (HBJ)—woodcuts

What Do You Say, Dear? by Sesyle Joslin; Illustrated by Maurice Sendak (Scott)—pen and ink with watercolor wash separations

Umbrella by Taro Yashima (Viking)—watercolor; pencil and brush for direct separations

1960

WINNER   *Nine Days to Christmas* by Marie Hall Ets and Aurora Labastida; Illustrated by Marie Hall Ets (Viking)—pencil on Dinobase

HONORS   *Houses from the Sea* by Alice E. Goudey; Illustrated by Adrienne Adams (Scribner)—watercolor (?)

The Moon Jumpers by Janice Udry; Illustrated by Maurice Sendak (Harper)—tempera

1961

WINNER   *Baboushka and the Three Kings* by Ruth Robbins; Illustrated by Nicolas Sidjakov (Parnassus)—tempera and felt-tip pen in four colors

HONOR   *Inch by Inch* by Leo Lionni (Obolensky)—rice paper collage and crayon

1962

WINNER   *Once a Mouse* by Marcia Brown (Scribner)—woodcuts and watercolor

HONORS   *The Fox Went Out on a Chilly Night;* Illustrated by Peter Spier (Doubleday)—pen and ink and watercolor on blue boards

Little Bear's Visit by Else Holmelund Minarik; Illustrated by Maurice Sendak (Harper)—pen and ink with wash separations

The Day We Saw the Sun Come Up by Alice E. Goudey; Illustrated by Adrienne Adams (Scribner)—graphite and gray wash with white gouache separations

1963

WINNER   *The Snowy Day* by Ezra Jack Keats (Viking)—collage: papers, paints, and gum-eraser stamps

HONORS   *The Sun Is a Golden Earring* by Natalia M. Belting; Illustrated by Bernarda Bryson (Holt)—pencil

Mr. Rabbit and the Lovely Present by Charlotte Zolotow; Illustrated by Maurice Sendak (Harper)—watercolor

1964

WINNER   *Where the Wild Things Are* by Maurice Sendak (Harper)—india ink line over full-color tempera

HONORS   *Swimmy* by Leo Lionni (Pantheon)—watercolor, rubber stamping, and pencil

All in the Morning Early by Sorche Nic Leodhas; Illustrated by Evaline Ness (Holt)—medium not known

Mother Goose and Nursery Rhymes; Illustrated by Philip Reed (Atheneum)—engravings on wood

1965

WINNER *May I Bring a Friend?* by Beatrice Schenk de Regniers; Illustrated by Beni Montresor (Atheneum)—pen-and-ink drawings on board in black with solid overlays and screened overlays on acetate

HONORS *Rain Makes Applesauce* by Julian Scheer; Illustrated by Marvin Bileck (Holiday)—pencil and watercolors (?)

The Wave by Margaret Hodges; Illustrated by Blair Lent (Houghton)—ink and cardboard cutouts

A Pocketful of Cricket by Rebecca Caudill; Illustrated by Evaline Ness (Holt)—medium not known

1966

WINNER *Always Room for One More* by Sorche Nic Leodhas; Illustrated by Nonny Hogrogian (Holt)—three-color preseparated art using pen for black line and pastels and wash for color

HONORS *Hide and Seek Fog* by Alvin Tresselt; Illustrated by Roger Duvoisin (Lothrop)—full-color gouache

Just Me by Marie Hall Ets (Viking)—paper batik

Tom Tit Tot by Evaline Ness (Holt)—woodcuts

1967

WINNER *Sam, Bangs & Moonshine* by Evaline Ness (Holt)—three-color preseparated art using Japanese pen and wash; printer's ink; roller; string

HONOR *One Wide River to Cross* by Barbara Emberley; Illustrated by Ed Emberley (Prentice)—woodcuts

1968

WINNER *Drummer Hoff* by Barbara Emberley; Illustrated by Ed Emberley (Prentice)—woodcuts and ink

HONORS *Frederick* by Leo Lionni (Pantheon)—collage with mixed media

Seashore Story by Yashima (Viking)—watercolor and pastel

The Emperor and the Kite by Jane Yolen; Illustrated by Ed Young (World)—paper cuts

1969

WINNER *The Fool of the World and the Flying Ship;* Retold by Arthur Ransome; Illustrated by Uri Shulevitz (Farrar)—pen and brush with black and colored inks

HONOR *Why the Sun and the Moon Live in the Sky* by Elphinstone Dayrell; Illustrated by Blair Lent (Houghton)—preseparated pen and ink in three colors

1970
WINNER   *Sylvester and the Magic Pebble* by William Steig (Windmill)—watercolor

HONORS   *Goggles!* by Ezra Jack Keats (Macmillan)—oil paint and collage

Alexander and the Wind-Up Mouse by Leo Lionni (Pantheon)—collage

Pop Corn and Ma Goodness by Edna Mitchell Preston; Illustrated by Robert Andrew Parker (Viking)—watercolor

Thy Friend, Obadiah by Brinton Turkle (Viking)—medium not known

The Judge by Harve Zemach; Illustrated by Margot Zemach (Farrar)—watercolor, pen and ink

1971
WINNER   *A Story A Story* by Gail E. Haley (Atheneum)—woodcuts

HONORS   *The Angry Moon* by William Sleator; Illustrated by Blair Lent (Atlantic/Little)—pen-and-ink drawings with acrylic glazes; full-color paintings

Frog and Toad Are Friends by Arnold Lobel (Harper)—pencil drawings in three colors

In the Night Kitchen by Maurice Sendak (Harper)—line drawings and wash

1972
WINNER   *One Fine Day* by Nonny Hogrogian (Macmillan)—acrylic paintings with turpentine on gesso panels

HONORS   *Hildilid's Night* by Cheli Duran Ryan; Illustrated byArnold Lobel (Macmillan)—pen-and-ink drawings with yellow overlays

If All the Seas Were One Sea by Janina Domanska (Macmillan)—etchings on zinc plates with brush-and-ink overlays

Moja Means One by Muriel Feelings; Illustrated by Tom Feelings (Dial)—graphite and paper collage

1973
WINNER   *The Funny Little Woman* by Arlene Mosel; Illustrated by Blair Lent (Dutton)—pen-and-ink line drawings with full-color acrylic glazes; full-color paintings

HONORS   *Anansi the Spider;* Adapted and illustrated by Gerald McDermott (Holt)—artwork preseparated in four colors with outline in ink

Hosie's Alphabet by Hosea, Tobias, and Lisa Baskin; Illustrated by Leonard Baskin (Viking)—watercolor

Snow White and the Seven Dwarfs; Translated by Randall Jarrell; Illustrated by Nancy Ekholm Burkert (Farrar)—brush and colored inks

When Clay Sings by Byrd Baylor; Illustrated by Tom Bahti (Scribner)—medium not known

1974
WINNER *Duffy and the Devil;* Retold by Harve Zemach; Pictures by Margot Zemach (Farrar)—pen-and-ink drawings with watercolor

HONORS *Three Jovial Huntsmen* by Susan Jeffers (Bradbury)—pen-and-ink drawings with wash overlays painted in oils

Cathedral by David Macaulay (Houghton)—pen and ink

1975
WINNER *Arrow to the Sun* by Gerald McDermott (Viking)—gouache and ink; black line preseparated

HONOR *Jambo Means Hello* by Muriel Feelings; Illustrated by Tom Feelings (Dial)—graphite and paper collage

1976
WINNER *Why Mosquitoes Buzz in People's Ears* by Verna Aardema; Pictures by Leo and Diane Dillon (Dial)—india ink; watercolor; pastels; vellum and frisket masks

HONORS *The Desert Is Theirs* by Byrd Baylor; Illustrated by Peter Parnall (Scribner)—pen and ink (?)

Strega Nona; Retold and illustrated by Tomie de Paola (Prentice)—watercolor and felt-tip pen over graphite

1977
WINNER *Ashanti to Zulu: African Traditions* by Margaret Musgrove; Pictures by Leo and Diane Dillon (Dial)—pastels, watercolors, and acrylics

HONORS *The Amazing Bone* by William Steig (Farrar)—watercolor (?)

The Contest; Retold and illustrated by Nonny Hogrogian (Greenwillow)—colored pencils and crayons for full color; pencil drawings for black and white

Fish for Supper by M. B. Goffstein (Dial)—ink drawings

The Golem by Beverly Brodsky McDermott (Lippincott)—gouache, watercolor, dye, and ink

Hawk, I'm Your Brother by Byrd Baylor; Illustrated by Peter Parnall (Scribner)—pen and ink (?)

1978

WINNER *Noah's Ark* by Peter Spier (Doubleday)—F pencil on paper; watercolor and white pencil; negatives scratched

HONORS *Castle* by David Macaulay (Houghton)—pen and ink

It Could Always Be Worse; Retold and illustrated by Margot Zemach (Farrar)—watercolor (?)

1979

WINNER *The Girl Who Loved Wild Horses* by Paul Goble (Bradbury)—full-color pen and ink and watercolor

HONORS *Freight Train* by Donald Crews (Greenwillow)—preseparated art; airbrush with transparent dyes

The Way to Start a Day by Byrd Baylor; Illustrated by Peter Parnall (Scribner)—pen and ink (?)

1980

WINNER *Ox-Cart Man* by Donald Hall; Pictures by Barbara Cooney (Viking) —acrylics on gesso-coated board

HONORS *Ben's Trumpet* by Rachel Isadora (Greenwillow)—pen and ink

The Garden of Abdul Gasazi by Chris Van Allsburg (Houghton)— carbon pencil on Strathmore paper

The Treasure by Uri Shulevitz (Farrar)—watercolor with black line on acetate

1981

WINNER *Fables* by Arnold Lobel (Harper)—gouache and pencil

HONORS *The Bremen-Town Musicians*; Retold and illustrated by Ilse Plume (Doubleday)—colored pencil and graphite (?)

The Grey Lady and the Strawberry Snatcher by Molly Bang (Four Winds)—watercolor, sometimes with white gouache undercoat on gray construction paper

Mice Twice by Joseph Low (McElderry/Atheneum)—watercolor and pen and ink (?)

Truck by Donald Crews (Greenwillow)—four halftone separations with black line drawings

1982

WINNER *Jumanji* by Chris Van Allsburg (Houghton)—conté pencil with conté dust

HONORS *Where the Buffaloes Begin* by Olaf Baker; Drawings by Stephen Gammell (Warne)—pencil drawings (?)

On Market Street by Arnold Lobel; Illustrated by Anita Lobel (Greenwillow)—watercolor and pen and ink

Outside over There by Maurice Sendak (Harper)—medium not known

A Visit to William Blake's Inn by Nancy Willard; Illustrated by Alice and Martin Provensen (HBJ)—medium not known

1983

WINNER *Shadow* by Blaise Cendrars; Translated and illustrated by Marcia Brown (Scribner)—collage: paper, woodcuts, acrylics

HONORS *A Chair for My Mother* by Vera Williams (Greenwillow)—watercolor

When I Was Young in the Mountains by Cynthia Rylant; Illustrated by Diane Goode (Dutton)—watercolor and fine-colored pencil

1984

WINNER *The Glorious Flight: Across the Channel with Louis Blériot* by Alice and Martin Provensen (Viking)—acrylic and pen and ink

HONORS *Little Red Riding Hood;* Retold and illustrated by Trina Schart Hyman (Holiday House)—ink and acrylic (?)

Ten, Nine, Eight by Molly Bang (Greenwillow)—gouache (poster paint)

1985

WINNER *Saint George and the Dragon;* Retold by Margaret Hodges; Illustrated by Trina Schart Hyman (Little, Brown)—india ink and acrylic

HONORS *Hansel and Gretel;* Retold by Rika Lesser; Illustrated by Paul O. Zelinsky (Dodd)—oil paintings

Have You Seen My Duckling? by Nancy Tafuri (Greenwillow)—watercolors and pastels

The Story of Jumping Mouse; Retold and illustrated by John Steptoe (Lothrop)—graphite pencil and india ink on paper

1986

WINNER *The Polar Express* by Chris Van Allsburg (Houghton)—full-color oil pastel on pastel paper

HONORS *The Relatives Came* by Cynthia Rylant; Illustrated by Stephen Gammell (Bradbury)—graphite and colored pencil

King Bidgood's in the Bathtub by Audrey Wood; Illustrated by Don Wood (HBJ)—oil on pressed wood (?)

1987

WINNER *Hey, Al* by Arthur Yorinks; Illustrated by Richard Egielski (Farrar) —watercolor

HONORS *The Village of Round and Square Houses* by Ann Grifalconi (Little, Brown)—pastels (?)

Alphabatics by Suse MacDonald (Bradbury)—cells, vinyl acrylic; gouache

Rumpelstiltskin; Retold and illustrated by Paul O. Zelinsky (Dutton)—oil paintings

1988

WINNER *Owl Moon* by Jane Yolen; Illustrated by John Schoenherr (Philomel)—pen and ink and watercolor

HONOR *Mufaro's Beautiful Daughters* by John Steptoe (Lothrop)—crosshatched pen and ink and watercolor

1989

WINNER *Song and Dance Man* by Karen Ackerman; Illustrated by Stephen Gammell (Knopf)—line drawings in colored pencil

HONORS *The Boy of the Three-Year Nap* by Dianne Snyder; Illustrated by Allen Say (Houghton)—brush-line, pen and ink, and watercolor

Free Fall by David Wiesner (Lothrop)—watercolor

Goldilocks and the Three Bears by James Marshall (Dial)—pen and ink and watercolor

Mirandy and Brother Wind by Patricia C. McKissack; Illustrated by Jerry Pinkney (Knopf)—pencil and watercolor

1990

WINNER *Lon Po Po* by Ed Young (Philomel)—watercolor and pastels

HONORS *Bill Peet: An Autobiography* by Bill Peet (Houghton)—pencil

Color Zoo by Lois Ehlert (Lippincott)—paper collage and die-cut forms

Hershel and the Hanukkah Goblins by Eric Kimmel; Illustrated by Trina Schart Hyman (Holiday House)—india ink and acrylic paint

The Talking Eggs by Robert San Souci; Illustrated by Jerry Pinkney (Dial)—pencil, colored-pencil, and watercolor

1991

WINNER *Black and White* by David Macaulay (Houghton) "Seeing Things" —watercolor "Problem Parents"—ink line and wash "A Waiting Game" —watercolor and gouache "Udder Confusion"—gouache paint

HONORS   *"More, More, More," Said the Baby: 3 Love Stories* by Vera B. Williams (Greenwillow)—gouache paints; lettering painted in watercolor based on Gill Sans Extra Bold Print

Puss in Boots by Fred Marcellino (di Capua/Farrar)—colored pencil on taupe textured illustration paper

1992
WINNER   *Tuesday* by David Wiesner (Clarion)—watercolor

HONOR   *Tar Beach* by Faith Ringgold (Crown)—acrylic on canvas

1993
WINNER   *Mirette on the High Wire* by Emily Arnold McCully (Putnam)—watercolor

HONORS   *Seven Blind Mice* by Ed Young (Philomel)—paper collage

The Stinky Cheese Man & Other Fairly Stupid Tales by Jon Scieszka; Illustrated by Lane Smith (Viking)—oil and mixed media

Working Cotton by Sherley Anne Williams; Illustrated by Carole Byard (HBJ)—acrylic on Stonehenge white paper

1994
WINNER   *Grandfather's Journey* by Allen Say (Houghton)—watercolor

HONORS   *Peppe the Lamplighter* by Elisa Bartone; Illustrated by Ted Lewin (Lothrop)—watercolor

In the Small, Small Pond by Denise Fleming (Holt)—colored cotton pulp poured through hand-cut stencils

Owen by Kevin Henkes (Greenwillow)—watercolor paints and black ink

Raven: A Trickster Tale from the Pacific Northwest by Gerald McDermott (Harcourt)—gouache, colored pencil, and pastel on heavyweight, cold-press watercolor paper

Yo! Yes? by Chris Raschka (Orchard)—watercolor and charcoal pencil

1995
WINNER   *Smoky Night* by Eve Bunting; Illustrated by David Diaz (Harcourt)—acrylic paintings set against mixed media collage backgrounds

HONORS   *Swamp Angel* by Anne Issacs; Illustrated by Paul O. Zelinsky (Dutton)—oil on cherry, maple, and birch veneers

John Henry by Julius Lester; Illustrated by Jerry Pinkney (Dial)—pencil, colored pencil, and watercolor

Time Flies by Eric Rohmann (Crown)—oil

1996

WINNER *Officer Buckle and Gloria* by Peggy Rathmann (Putnam)—watercolor and ink

HONORS *Alphabet City* by Stephen T. Johnson (Viking)—pastels, watercolors, gouache, and charcoal on hot pressed watercolor paper

Zin! Zin! Zin! a Violin by Lloyd Moss; Illustrated by Marjorie Priceman (Simon & Schuster)—gouache

The Faithful Friend by Robert D. San Souci; Illustrated by Brian Pinkney (Simon & Schuster)—scratchboard and oil

Tops & Bottoms adapted and illustrated by Janet Stevens (Harcourt)—watercolor, colored pencil, and gesso on paper made by hand by Ray Tomasso, Denver, Colorado

1997

WINNER *Golem* by David Wisniewski (Clarion)—color-aid, coral, and bark cut papers

HONORS *Hush! A Thai Lullaby* by Minfong Ho; Illustrated by Holly Meade (Orchard)—cut-paper collage with ink

The Graphic Alphabet by David Pelletier (Orchard)—computer-generated images reproduced in full color

The Paperboy by Dav Pilkey (Orchard)—acrylics and india ink

Starry Messenger by Peter Sís (Farrar Straus Giroux)—pen and brown ink and watercolor

1998

WINNER *Rapunzel* by Paul O. Zelinsky (Dutton)—oil reproduced in full color

HONORS *The Gardener* by Sarah Stewart; Illustrated by David Small (Farrar)—watercolor, ink pen line, and crayon

Harlem by Walter Dean Myers; Illustrated by Christopher Myers (Scholastic)—ink, gouache, and cut-paper collage

There Was an Old Lady Who Swallowed a Fly by Simms Taback (Viking)—mixed media and collage on kraft paper in color

1999

WINNER *Snowflake Bentley* by Jacqueline Briggs Martin; Illustrated by Mary Azarian (Houghton Mifflin)—woodcuts, hand-tinted with watercolors

HONORS *Duke Ellington* by Andrea Davis Pinkney; Illustrated by Brian Pinkney (Hyperion)—scratchboard renderings with gouache, luma dyes, and oil paint

No, David! by David Shannon (Blue Sky/Scholastic)—acrylics and colored pencil

Snow by Uri Shulevitz (Farrar Straus Giroux)—ink and watercolor washes

Tibet: Through the Red Box by Peter Sís (Farrar Straus Giroux)—watercolor, pen and ink, and oil pastel

SOME USEFUL DEFINITIONS

Acetate—a clear, plastic film used for overlays.

Airbrush—a mechanical painting tool that emits a fine spray of liquid or ink.

Batik—a wax-resistant process in which the design or image is first painted on the surface in wax so that, when the surface is dyed, the wax sections will not take the color.

Binder—the ingredient of a paint that holds together the particles of pigment and fixes them into a continuous film as the paint dries.

Color preseparation—the process by which an artist prepares, manually, the art to be printed in a four-, three-, or two-color book. This is done by preparing a master preseparation and overlays, each specifying a color to be reproduced for the image(s) contained in the area of the picture. When all of the overlays are printed together, the colors form the final picture.

Conté pencil—square-sectioned drawing chalks in black, white, sanguine, and sepia.

Dinobase—acetate sand-blasted to roughen the surface, making it similar to a lithographic stone; no longer used.

Dye—a coloring agent soluble in liquid that imparts color to a surface by being absorbed.

Engraving—any process by which a linear design is made on the surface of a hard and durable substance.

F pencil—a medium-hard graphite pencil.

Four-color process—a printing process in which the full range of the colors of an image is reproduced by means of four separate printing plates (black, blue, red, and yellow), which can be separated via camera, computer, or artist. After the separations, the plates are printed one on top of another in transparent process inks, as dictated by the separations, to create the final picture.

Frisket mask—a thin paper placed over an area not to be colored during painting or airbrushing.

Graphite—a carbon in stick form used for drawing.

India ink—a permanent black ink made of lampblack and glue binder.

Linoleum cuts—a relief printing process in which the image or design is cut into the surface of a block of linoleum.

Lithograph—a print made by drawing on limestone or a zinc plate with a greasy material, then wetting the plate and applying greasy ink that will only adhere to the drawn line. Dampened paper is then rubbed over the stone with a special press to create the final print. A *lithographic crayon* or *pencil* is often used for drawing on the *lithographic stone*, which is a block of limestone with its surface ground so an image can be made upon it. In *offset lithography*, the image is first transferred to an intermediate surface (a rubber blanket) before it is transferred to the paper.

Overlay—a transparent or translucent film attached to artwork carrying additional detail to be reproduced.

Paint—a substance consisting of a pigment evenly dispersed in a liquid which, when applied to a surface as a fluid, dries into a continuous film of color. In *acrylic* paint, the pigment is dispersed in an emulsion binder that is a liquid form of acrylic resin. In *oil* paint, the pigment is dispersed in a drying oil (usually linseed). In *watercolor*, the finely ground pigment is dispersed in a water-soluble gum binder and is transparent; *gouache* is a watercolor that uses opaque rather than transparent colors; *tempera* is an opaque watercolor paint in which the pigment is ground in water and mixed with egg yolk; it can also be *poster paint*.

Pastels—a drawing medium consisting of pigment mixed with gum binder, rolled or compressed into stick form.

Pigment—a finely ground colored powder that may be mixed with a liquid vehicle to make paint.

Scratchboard—an ink technique in which a white board is covered with india ink and a design or image is scratched into it.

Wash—an application of ink or watercolor heavily diluted with water to form a thin film of transparent color.

Woodcut—a relief printing process in which the image or design is cut into the surface of a plank-grain wood block.

Bibliography

Children's Books: 1955–1957. New York: American Institute of Graphic Arts, 1958.

Children's Books: 1958–1960. New York: American Institute of Graphic Arts, 1960.

Children's Books: 1961–1962. New York: American Institute of Graphic Arts, 1962.

Cianciolo, Patricia J., ed. *Picture Books for Children.* 4th ed. American Library Assn., 1997.

de Angeli, Marguerite. *Butter at the Old Price.* Garden City: Doubleday, 1971.

Illustrations for Children: The Gladys English Collection. Sacramento: California Library Assn., Gladys English Memorial Collection Committee, 1963.

Jones, Helen. *Robert Lawson, Illustrator.* Boston: Little, 1972.

Kingman, Lee, and others. *Illustrators of Children's Books, 1957–1966*. Boston: Horn Book, 1968.

Kingman, Lee, ed. *Newbery and Caldecott Medal Books: 1956–1965*. Boston: Horn Book, 1965.

Kingman, Lee, ed. *Newbery and Caldecott Medal Books: 1966–1975*. Boston: Horn Book, 1975.

Kingman, Lee, ed. *Newbery and Caldecott Medal Books: 1976–1985*. Boston: Horn Book, 1986.

Lanes, Selma G. *The Art of Maurice Sendak*. New York: Abrams, 1980.

Larkin, David, ed. *The Art of Nancy Ekholm Burkert*. New York: Harper, 1977.

Lucie-Smith, Edward. *The Thames and Hudson Dictionary of Art Terms*. London: Thames & Hudson, 1984.

Martin, Judy. *The Longman Dictionary of Art*. Harlow, Eng.: Longman Group, 1986.

Miller, Bertha Mahony, and others. *Caldecott Medal Books: 1938–1957*. Boston: Horn Book, 1957.

Quick, John. *Artists' and Illustrators' Encyclopedia, II ed*. New York: McGraw-Hill, 1977.

Shulevitz, Uri. *Writing with Pictures*. New York: Watson-Guptill, 1985.

Viguers, Ruth Hill, and others. *Illustrators of Children's Books, 1946–1956*. Boston: Horn Book, 1958.

Also consulted: all issues of *Horn Book Magazine*: 1938–1986.

Author / Illustrator Index

Title Index